Little Steps to Big Achievements

How To Develop Habits And Shape Your Life With 10-Minute Actions

By D J Pinkney

Little Steps to Big Achievement

HOW TO DEVELOP HABITS AND SHAPE YOUR LIFE WITH 10 MINUTE ACTIONS

AUTHOR
D J PINKNEY

CO-AUTHOR
MYRA MUILI

EDITOR
MAWRA WAZIR

ILLUSTRATIONS BY
NATALIA TUTANOVA

D J Pinkney

About This Book

This book is about taking small steps that can lead to big success. It focuses on the techniques & things you can implement every day, for only ten minutes to change your life. It goes in-depth on how to do each one of them, providing actionable steps to get started.

gain clarity, momentum, and consistency

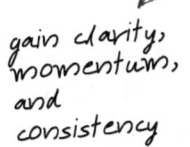

small steps

Develop Habits

10 Minutes a Day

Table of Contents

"The man who removes a mountain begins
by carrying away small stones."

- Confucius, Chinese philosopher

Introduction

Do you dream big?

Me too.

I dream of traveling all over the world. I dream of being the fittest I can be and sustaining that throughout my lifetime. I dream of riding a dragon to save Mordor. Well, not really, but you get the idea. I have big dreams. I also have the confidence that as big as my dreams are, I can achieve them all. I know that because I have achieved dreams that seemed too big for me, and because I know the secret to attain big dreams.

I'm a person who used to jump from one thing to the next. I would always start something and never finish it. I remember the many false starts I had with going to the gym and resolving to read a book a month and never seeing it through. I recall all the times I started learning new skills never to see them through. It was mortifying.

That is, until I learned that most big ideas are not accomplished in the short term. They take persistence and consistency, and the journey to fulfilling them is built on small steps. It's the small steps that allow you to see the progress you're making toward your goals each day. When I stumbled on this truth, I realized that you're more likely to stick with something when you can take small steps toward it. What a revelation this was – to realize that true success is not born from one humongous lucky step, but out of daily consistent small steps.

Just think about it: do you remember a time when you were afraid to take the first step toward a lofty goal? When you were scared to start your own small business, or when you were too tired to come up with yet another workout routine that you were sure you would never be able to stick to? Why was that?

Chances are it was because the journey to accomplish that goal appeared too big that it was overwhelming. The road appeared blurry and very long, and the goal was too far away. You thought there was too much to do, and you could not exactly see a clear path toward the goal. Or maybe, you got caught up in wanting to see immediate results, and that distracted you from putting in a daily effort.

The thing with big dreams is that they're not accomplished in one day. There's no such thing as an overnight success. You don't need one huge, monumental effort to achieve your goal, and that should be liberating. You now have the freedom to take it one day at a time.

The only way to accomplish goals that are big and ambitious – the kind of goals that will change your life forever - is by consistently taking one tiny step at a time in the direction of those goals. I know, it almost sounds too good to be true. In our bigger-is-better culture of su-persize meals, IMAX movies, and extreme makeovers, it seems nearly impossible to see how small steps can create big changes, but they can.

Let me tell you Lydia's story. Like most of us, when Lydia went to school, she got drilled with the notion that good performance means knowing the answers to every question, turning in factually correct assignments, and getting the best grades. She learned that we're measured by these factors – pass or fail. Distinction. Due to this concept that she was taught since her childhood, she believed that IQ was the key to success in life, and you either had it or you didn't.

When she finished her undergraduate degree in Busi-ness Administration, she stepped into the job market, determined to make bills like everyone else, ready to start a family and advance her career. She landed a job as a sales representative in a prestigious insurance firm in California. She was not fully satisfied with this being her path in life, but could she dare hope for more? After all, she didn't have the IQ she knew to be everything. Her educational system's conditioning had influenced how she compared her ability to succeed against others. Unintentionally, it made her put an unnecessary emphasis on IQ whenever she would set goals and judge her ability to achieve them, and she never bothered to consider other factors, because in her mind, it wouldn't matter.

One day, her friend invited her to a book club. They were discussing a classic by Hemingways in a small library in town, and she was not as engaged with the discussion as she would've wanted. She started browsing other options on the shelves and by chance, she came across an old book that she found interesting.

She wasn't allowed to take that book home for some reason, so she decided to read it right there after her group discussion was over. When she was finally on her own, Lydia opened the old book and read a few pages. That's where she discovered the idea of taking small steps and how they can work wonders. When she got home, she decided to research it, and before long, she was intrigued to try this new idea in her own life. It was like a new ray of hope for her.

Lydia convinced herself that she had nothing to lose by trying to put this idea into practice. She knew she wanted to be an author someday, but she didn't have the skills yet to make that dream a reality. After thinking about it for a while, Lydia enrolled in a writing course online. She gave the course only 10 minutes of her time every day. That was all she could spare.

Soon enough, she noticed that she was making progress. She was learning how to brainstorm ideas and how to arrange them well. She was starting to improve her writing skills. She no longer struggled to create adequate emails at work, for example. Long story short, in a period of six months, Lydia had the skills she needed to author a book and had started working on a manuscript. She no longer believed that being smart gets you further. The much stronger indicator of your potential is your consistency, perseverance, and ability to take continuous small steps without fail.

The key to fulfilling our dreams lies in the little progress we make every day. Of course, the amount of steps we will have to take to achieve those goals will depend on the magnitude of the goal. If most people fail to achieve their goals, it's not because life is unfair, or because they don't have the right IQ. It's because they fail to take the necessary small steps toward those goals.

The difference between people who are successful and those who are not isn't luck, IQ, or privilege. It's commitment. It's true that there are people who have things easier than others, but that should never be an excuse to put down your weapons and give up fighting for your goals. Rather, it should fire you up and motivate you to keep moving forward.

Do you know what happens when we take it one step at a time? We get a sense of achievement and satisfaction.

Our brain registers both big and small victories the same, so each accomplishment, regardless of how small it is, floods your body and mind with serotonin, the chemical in your brain that's responsible for creating strong positive emotions and keeping you happy. It leaves you feeling better about yourself and boosts your self-confidence. And when you have self-confidence, nothing can stop you.

Let's say you want to lose weight. To reach your target weight, you need to lose 10kg. Imagine you divide that big goal into smaller goals. For example, you decide to lose 1kg per week. This way, your current goal becomes easier and more achievable, preventing you from getting overwhelmed or exhausted by just the idea of a big scary goal.

Once you have a current goal that's small and manageable for you, you can set up the steps you need to take to achieve it. Maybe all you need to do to lose 1kg a week is to change what you eat. Maybe you just need to replace your sugar with a healthier sweetener like Stevia, or start by walking 5,000 steps per day. Whatever the goal, it's now small enough to do without folding, and it gets you closer to your overall goal every day.

That's the magic of small steps.

All changes, even the positive ones, are scary. That's why when we attempt to reach our goals through revolutionary or radical means, we often fail. Those means overwhelm us and increase our fear. Small steps disarm the fear response in the brain, stimulating creative play and rational thought. They let you tiptoe past the amygdala toward the kind of life you want for yourself.

When I learned the power of small steps, I started to implement them in my life. I soon found out that doing the very same things for 10 minutes each day could have a big impact on my life. It could help me finally reach my goals. So, instead of trying to go to the gym for an hour a day, I started doing a 10-minute HIIT workout and went for 10-minute walks.

Within two weeks, I started seeing changes. I was getting way closer to my fitness goals than I ever had with my previous attempts. As I was looking at academic literature and journals to understand what was happening to me, I learned that we all naturally settle into a daily set of habits that make our comfort zones.

These comfort zones are resilient. They have the ability to rebuff our efforts to make changes in how we live, especially big changes. At the beginning of each year, we make resolutions; we plan to quit smoking, go on a diet, and lose weight. Then, in a few weeks, we are back to our habits.

Why is that?

Very few of us have the resolve and the discipline to make big changes quickly – or at all. We get stuck in our comfort zones, whether those are healthy or unhealthy. We just cannot seem to change, and so after a couple of days of trying, we give up.

Giving only 10 minutes a day to do a HIIT workout was working wonders for me because it wasn't too lofty of a goal. It was empowering me to change my routine gradually.

The good news is, anyone can do that. You can make a small change in your routine today and stick to it. With small changes, your subconscious mind, which guards your comfort zone, doesn't notice and act to stop them. Gradually, these small changes will transform into big shifts in your comfort zone.

Today, I still have a comfort zone, but most of the habits and routines that make it up are good, and they're pushing me toward my big dreams.

That's the idea of this book. By taking 10 minutes every day to make a small change, you're gradually changing your behaviors and routines, and transforming your comfort zone for the better. All the changes I recommend in this book have worked well for me. They have allowed me to stop stressing and ruminating and actually put in the work to change my life. After years of practicing them, I'm more focused and able to make important choices in my life, and you will too.

By simply setting a 10-minute time limit on each of these tasks, I was able to stick to them without them feeling like a chore. Not only that, but I was also able to stick to each task every day. I got to do things I wouldn't have been able to do in the past.

Today, I'm building an online informational and publishing business because of this very same idea. I'm ticking things off my bucket list faster than ever before. Every day, I still read a book for 10 minutes. I still work out daily. I do these things because of that foundation of small steps. That's the knowledge I want to pass on with this book.

It doesn't matter what your goal is – getting fitter, stronger, starting a business, finally learning how to read, getting better at math, or quitting your 9-5. Whatever the goal, this book is for you. It's like your mentor, ready to hold your hand as you walk on the path to achieving your big dreams, one small task a day. If that sounds like what you are looking for, keep reading.

Chapter 1:
The Science Behind Habits

In order to make a change to your daily life pattern, it's important to understand how exactly that pattern works and what you can do to start that change in a healthy and potentially long-term way. To do that, we first need to study the science behind habits and how they work.

How Habits are Formed

Have you ever taken a moment to consider all your habits or the way they influence your daily life? Have you ever found yourself trying to change a habit to adapt to a new environment? How easy or difficult was it?

Psychologists say that a habit is formed when a new behavior becomes automated and is enacted with the least possible conscious awareness. That's because habits are typically etched into our neural pathways. Habits can also be described as our brain's automatic actions or reactions. For example, how many times in a day do you reach for your phone to read emails, scroll on Instagram, or check your Facebook?

While some habits are harmless, some can be detrimental. Wasting an hour each time you get on Twitter, for example, might be more unhealthy than it's productive. However, if a habit is good, it can also benefit you a great deal. Learning to brush our teeth when we were kids and making a habit out of it gives us the advantage of good dental health for the rest of our lives. Similarly, making a habit of doing a 30-minute walk five times a week will improve your physical health, keep you in shape, and give you a boost of endorphins, keeping you happy and content.

Habits make your life. How everything in your life works today is because of your habits. If you're in shape, you can link that to your habits. At the same time, how happy or unhappy you are and how successful or unsuccessful you are, it all draws from your habits.

The things you do repeatedly ultimately make you the kind of person you are. One of the likely reasons we have habits as humans are because habits are efficient. They allow us to perform useful tasks without wasting energy and time deliberating about them. This is the tendency we want to lean into and maximize.

To do this, we have to step back and look at the way habits are formed.

The process of habit formation can either be intentional or unintentional. We form countless habits as we move through life, sometimes without being aware that we're doing it. Because they have a knee-jerk nature, they get our needs met more efficiently in our daily life.

In his best-selling book *The Power of Habit*, Charles Duhigg explains that there's a general framework for understanding the way habits work, which can help you as you work on changing them. Some habits are easier to analyze and influence while others tend to be obstinate and complex, sometimes never fully changing.

This is how Duhigg explains the habit loop in his book.

Cue - Craving - Routine - Reward

The process of changing a habit begins with identifying the behavior that you want to embody, experimenting with rewards, so that they help you change your behavior, and then finding a cue for the behavior.

Every habit is formed through learning and repetition. You develop habits in pursuit of a goal by starting to associate specific cues with a behavioral response that meets the goal. Over time, your thoughts of the behavior, and eventually the behavior itself, get triggered by those cues.

To make it simpler, think of the process of habit formation as happening in these four steps – cue, craving, routine, and reward. Breaking the process down into its basic parts helps us understand what makes a habit, its functioning, and how to change it. These four steps are the backbone for every habit you can think about, and your brain goes through them in the same order every time.

1. Cue

The cue is a trigger that causes your brain to start a certain behavior. It is the information that predicts a certain reward. It launches your brain into automatic mode and tells it which habit to use for a certain reward.

In prehistoric times, our ancestors were responding to cues that signaled the location of primary rewards like water, sex, and food. Today, we also respond to cues that predict secondary rewards such as fame, money, praise, status, approval, friendship, love, and power.

In simpler examples, if we make a habit of eating a doughnut each time we pass a doughnut box in our house, grabbing a heavy snack each time we open our refrigerator, or getting a big greasy burger each time we feel stressed, these actions quickly turn into habits. Because all we need to eat unhealthily is a little cue. In these examples, the cues are passing a doughnut box, opening a refrigerator, and feeling stressed, respectively.

Simple cues like these control our habit loops and are the basis of habit formation.

2. Craving

Cravings motivate every habit. If there's no desire or motivation – craving a change – there's no reason to do anything. At this stage of the habit loop, what you're craving is not the habit, but the change in the state that it will give you, and this is true both for positive and negative habits.

For example, you don't crave a cigarette, you crave the feeling of relief you get after taking one. You're not motivated to brush your teeth for the sake of it, but by the feeling of a clean mouth. You don't turn the TV on for the sake of turning it on, you're looking for entertainment.

Each craving is tied to a desire to see your internal state change.

Cravings are different for each person. Theoretically speaking, any information or cue can trigger a craving. In practice, however, people don't get motivated by the same cues. Someone who's addicted to gambling may be triggered by the sound of slot machines, but the same sounds are just noise to someone else.

3. Routine/Response

Routine is the third step in the habit formation loop, which refers to the main action or thought that you perform in response to a cue and the craving it causes. Whether you get to the third step depends on how motivated you are and how much resistance there is to the response. If a certain action demands more mental or physical effort than you are willing to put in, then you will not take it.

How you respond is also a function of your ability. It sounds obvious, but you can only form a habit if you are capable of performing the action. If your desire is the prestige of dunking a basketball, you can't act on it if you cannot jump high enough to reach the hoop.

4. Reward

The reward is the end goal of each action or habit loop. The cue hints at the reward, the craving wants the reward, and the routine is about getting the reward. It's the reward that helps your brain comprehend if the habit loop is worth remembering for the future.

As a general rule, a reward either satisfies or teaches. A reward can also exist just to satisfy your craving. Here, I'm talking about general things, like water and food, which give us the energy we need to go about our day.

While on the other hand, getting a promotion brings you respect and more money, which is better than some basic needs. Similarly, getting in shape improves your mental and physical health and increases your dating prospects. But the more immediate benefit of these rewards is that they satisfy your craving to gain status or win approval. For a moment, the reward gives you contentment and relief from the craving.

More than that, rewards teach us which actions are worth remembering. Your brain is wired in such a way that it detects rewards. As you operate in your daily life, your sensory nervous system continually monitors the actions that satisfy your desires and offer pleasure. Feelings of disappointment and pleasure form part of your feedback mechanism so that your brain uses them to tell between useful actions and unhealthy ones. The purpose of rewards is to complete the habit cycle and close the habit loop.

If you're trying to form a new habit with different steps, and it's lacking in any of these four stages, it won't work. Without a cue, the habit will never begin. Reduce the craving, and you will never be motivated to take action. Make the task difficult, and you will never be able to do it. If the reward does not satisfy your desire, there will be no reason to repeat the action in the future. Without the first three steps, you'll take no action. Without the fourth, you won't repeat the behavior.

Psychologists refer to the above four steps as the habit loop. These stages create an endless cycle that is ever-running as long as you're alive. Your brain is ever scanning the environment, guessing what will happen next, trying out a number of responses, and learning from the responses.

Some researchers have actually split the four steps into two phases – the problem and the solution phase. The craving and cue make the problem phase while the reward and routine make the solution phase. In the problem phase, you realize the need for change while in the solution phase, you take action and get the desired change.

The idea behind this classification is that all behavior is about solving a problem. Sometimes, the problem is that you have seen something good and you want it. Other times, the problem is a pain you're experiencing that you want relief from.

Remember that these stages don't always happen slowly and one by one. Sometimes they can seem to bleed into each other. For example, what do you do when your phone buzzes? You grab it and read the text. The buzz is the cue. The craving is to learn the contents of the message, picking up your phone is the routine, and the reward is reading the message. Yet, these steps happen in a matter of seconds.

In another scenario, you smell hot dogs as you walk down the street to your office. The smell makes you crave a hot dog. You get the hot dog and eat it, satisfying your craving. In time, buying the hot dog becomes associated with walking the street near your office.

This breakdown can be done for any habit. It's not something that you do occasionally, but an endless loop that is always active and running – even now, as you read this book. The whole process takes a split second, and we use it continually without realizing it. Imagine entering a dark room and turning on the lights. You've done the simple habit so many times that it's automated, yet you still go through the four stages, just in a shorter time.

By the time we become adults, we hardly notice the habits which run our lives, but they're always there. Many of us hardly ever give a second thought to the fact that we wear the same shoe first every time, switch off the light when we leave a room, or change into other clothes after returning home from work. After years of mental programming, we thoughtlessly slip into these patterns.

This book allows you to use the habit formation loop to design good habits and get rid of bad ones by setting aside only 10 minutes each day per the desired habit.

I've found the loop very useful because it makes the process of habit formation effortless. All you have to do is make the good habit you want to form seem obvious, attractive, easy, and satisfying.

This is where little steps come in. They play into the habit formation loop, by making the routine easy. Taking only 10 minutes on the little steps makes the reward satisfying. The spirit of this book works alongside the grain of human nature, rather than working against it.

The Power of Small Steps

I've become convinced over time that small steps create a tremendous ripple effect. They help us to get started. Most of us don't have trouble with the first two steps of the habit formation loop. We can easily notice the things that we need to change in our lives, and we recognize how this change would benefit us.

The problem comes with the routine. And a focus on small steps overcomes this problem. It helps us to get started because small steps make the routine less overwhelming. Fortunately, once you get started, inertia takes over and you find it easier to keep going.

No wonder many philosophers agree that the biggest hindrance to achieving great things is often the beginning. Mark Twain is quoted to have said, *'The secret to being ahead is beginning.'*

For years, I imagined myself being someone who meditated regularly, but I couldn't imagine investing one hour every day the way Gandhi is said to have done. Thankfully, I eventually learned that only 10 minutes a day could do the trick. With that small commitment, I was able to develop the restorative habit of meditation. Nowadays, I simply turn to a quieter corner and easily clear my mind.

Small steps allow us to focus on the immediate next step. Imagine you're an athlete. Small steps are akin to just focusing on wearing your running shoes, opening your door, getting on the track, running 100 meters, and then the next step, until eventually you're done with your tough workout.

More to that, small steps compound. They make big results. Whether you're renovating your kitchen, building your endurance, or preparing for your next big presentation, small steps add up.

Think of fitness, for instance. A team of researchers from Columbia University was studying how short periods of exercise affected the participants of the study. They found that people who exercised only 10 minutes per session three days a week for two months, had almost the same strength improvements as people who exercised for more than one hour per session.

A similar study from Chicago University found that people who cycled for 10 minutes on three days of the week saw gains similar to those who cycled for 50 minutes.

The results are replicable with any habit. Whatever it is, small steps compound, and not only that but succeeding at a little step breeds more success. Similarly with compound interest, little steps make for impressive successes. Done well, small steps are too small to fail at, which means that you succeed every time at completing the small task.

Once you start succeeding at them, the feel-good hormones and chemicals from succeeding make it easier to continue. Small steps minimize your risk while increasing your chances of success. Each step gives you a chance to learn and adjust while at the same time reassuring you that no one step will destroy the goodwill you have worked hard to build.

Small steps help us to create habits consistently. As Olin Miller put it, *'If you want to make any job look difficult, keep postponing it.'*

With small steps, you avoid decision fatigue. They allow you to manage your cognitive load better, which gives you more headspace to handle everything else. They help you manage your distractions as well, making consistency easy and making it more likely that you resist the urge to postpone. Then, as you see your progress, it builds momentum, which translates to higher productivity and creativity. Whenever you are beginning a new thing, feeling assured that it's achievable is important, and small steps give you that sense of attainability because they are not overwhelming.

As it is, small steps are more likely to stick. They're easier to fit into overscheduled and hectic days, which if we can admit, most of us face on a regular basis. Small attainable steps boost your confidence. The added bonus is that small, incremental changes actually stick because, unlike sudden, radical transformations, they have staying power.

How to Make the Best Use of This Book

In this chapter, you understand the basic principles that make each one of the 13 habits provided in this book work. You have an argument for beginning small and for only setting aside 10 minutes of your day for each of the changes you want to make.

Even so, 13 habits are still quite many, and going at them all at the same time goes against the very idea of this book. That's why I recommend that you pick two to four habits, to begin with. Better yet, you can use the rule of three. According to the rule of three, each day, you have to act on three specific habits that move you closer to your goal. It doesn't matter how small these actions seem, as long as they're directed toward your goal and are actually in the right direction.

By the rule of three, you would only choose three of the small steps recommended in this book and work on them until they become a habit, before you can move to the next ones. The idea is that whatever the goal, taking three steps each day will eventually create major progress, often in less time than you can imagine. Individually, each small step may not appear that important, but they add up over time to create extraordinary results. By committing to making small progress every day, you turn an otherwise difficult challenge into something doable.

Because one of the hardest parts of making habits is repetition, make sure that you make your three habits a non-negotiable part of your daily schedule. Do not give in to the urge to postpone or brush them off because they seem small.

While you're at it, make sure you track your progress. Keep a record of the activities you do each day, and review them every fortnight. When your journey involves taking small steps across time, it's easy to overlook everything you're actually accomplishing. Take time every fortnight to review what you've done, and you'll be amazed at how far you've come. This will motivate you to keep going.

10 MINUTES A DAY FOR YOUR BODY

Chapter 2:
Go Outside to Improve Your Overall Health

When work gets very busy, many of us don't prioritize spending time outside.

Why should I leave my office when I have fast deadlines and a lot of wo"rk? We ask.

But taking 10 minutes out of your busy schedule to go for a walk or spend time in nature can be all the relief you need from the stress of your work day. It can do wonders for your mood, your ability to finish tasks, and your overall health.

Research shows that one of the most harmful things we can do to our health is to live a sedentary lifestyle. A sedentary lifestyle increases the risks of negative cardiovascular outcomes such as heart attacks and strokes.

It's also a risk factor for many other medical conditions. Whether you take a walk at lunchtime or run in your neighborhood while doing an errand, getting sunshine and fresh air is good for you.

Nature Is Medicine

Research shows that in the US, adolescents and adults spend more than 90% of their time indoors. Most of that time is spent in front of a screen. The numbers are pretty similar in other parts of the world. Too much screen time and not nearly enough time spent in nature has been confirmed to contribute to negative mental health outcomes, such as anxiety and depression, while spending time in nature has many mental health benefits, like better sleep, reduced stress, and greater happiness. Numerous research studies have explored the different positive effects of nature on our physical and mental well-being.

One research that was published by the University of Tokyo found that the benefits of spending some time in nature are more than previously believed. In the study, researchers reviewed more than 300 academic articles from 62 countries on CESs (cultural ecosystem services), otherwise referred to as the intangible or non-material contributions to well-being provided by nature.

They found 227 unique pathways that connect one CES to a single constituent of well-being, which is many more links than was assumed earlier. According to the research, connecting with nature gives opportunities for leisure, recreation, personal development, spiritual fulfillment, aesthetic experiences, and social relations.

Previous studies have proven that spending some time in nature can give benefits like enhanced mental and physical health, a sense of place, and social cohesion. Besides the 227 pathways identified at the University of Tokyo, there are 16 different mechanisms involved in the link between nature and health. These mechanisms are the general types of connections through which more pathways are created. Some of these mechanisms include cohesive, formative, transcendent, and satisfaction.

The cohesive mechanism is responsible for developing meaningful human relations via interactions with nature, the formative has to do with things like attitude, mood, and behaviors that change over a short time or instantly upon interacting with nature. The satisfaction mechanism refers to your needs and expectations getting met when you interact with nature, while the transcendent refers to other benefits related to your spiritual or religious values.

The findings from Tokyo University provide a way to systematize the curative effects of being in nature. They provide a united information base and a conceptual framework for the way nature heals us. However, they're not necessarily surprising.

Separate research has proven that by spending only 10 minutes a day in nature, you can boost your self-esteem and mood. Those few minutes of fresh air can leave you feeling better. A study conducted at the University of Essex found that spending that time doing 'green exercise' or simply an activity in nature can boost your self-esteem.

The most striking thing about these findings was that the 10-minute dose proved to be more effective than spending more than 60 minutes or half a day outside. The group that spent more time outside experienced smaller positive self-esteem and mood changes compared to those who only went outside for 10 minutes. This is to say that you can meaningfully gain from just taking a walk around your office building or strolling down the block for 10 minutes.

Not only that but in those 10 minutes, you can get a dose of vitamin D that your body needs. Research from Harvard Medical School has found that the majority of people in the US are not getting enough vitamin D which they need to maintain a strong immune system and fight disease. Deficiencies in vitamin D are a real threat for most of us who work desk jobs, given that we don't prioritize getting some sunlight during our busy work days. Fortunately, you can go outside for only 10 minutes a day and help deal with this problem. Spending only 10 minutes in the sun increases the number of white blood cells in your body, which strengthens your immunity. Vitamin D is also important for your muscles, bones, and teeth to remain healthy.

Spending only 10 minutes a day in nature will help you feel less stressed. It doesn't matter what those 10 minutes look like as long as you are outside - it could be spent meeting with a co-worker or having lunch outside.

Being outside also lowers your stress hormone levels. Researchers at the University of Michigan wanted to understand what the sweet spot is for spending time outside and getting the benefits of stress relief. They found that you get the greatest payoff in terms of lowering your cortisol levels if you spend a maximum of 10 minutes sitting or walking in a place that gives you a sense of nature.

Being outside can also help you with weight management. If you're struggling to lose weight, spending more time outdoors could be the answer. Stress reduction will help you in your efforts to lose weight. Stress generally erodes self-control, making it hard for you to keep healthy habits, so when you start feeling overwhelmed, you can simply go outside.

Many studies have also documented the benefits of outdoor time on vision improvement. Your ocular health will thank you for spending 10 minutes a day outside. That exercise interrupts the sustained screen time and gives your eyes a much-needed break. It also improves your attention span and your short-term memory. Research involving people who reported suffering from mental fatigue found that spending only 10 minutes on a short walk eased their suffering and made them feel fresher.

Perhaps, the most significant benefit of going outside is that it yields healthier hearts. Walking will get your blood flowing. It will reduce your cholesterol levels, blood sugar, and blood pressure, which can help you if you're fighting type 2 diabetes, for example.

Besides, you'll feel more energized by just going outside because it activates your whole system, so you'll feel more energy. Some experts refer to it as taking 'micro-breaks.' These breaks are particularly helpful if you don't have a lot of time to spare out of your busy schedule. A 10-minute break is an easy way to perk yourself up.

10 Minutes a Day Outside

You don't have to set aside a very specific 10 minutes out of your day to go outside, even though that can be helpful. You can also respond to your daily needs and schedule by taking the break at a time when you deem it most convenient.

The idea is for you to find a pattern that fits into your lifestyle. You can go to the park in the evening as you walk your dog or you can walk around your building as you go to get a cup of tea, whatever it looks like is up to you. Even an activity like shopping at your local grocery store or at Costco can count as time outside. As a rule of thumb, begin a timer every time you go outside. You want to make sure that you get to at least 10 minutes.

If you find yourself struggling, you can mix up your 10-minute nature walk to make it more engaging for you. Alternatively, you can choose times in your day when the walk will be most helpful to you. Going for a walk first thing in the morning, for example, can help you wake up and plan your day accordingly. You can have your meetings outside and make them walking meetings rather than sitting meetings. You can take a walk over lunchtime to give yourself a much-needed break. Some people even go as far as taking public transportation up to a certain point and then walking the last part – whatever you need to do to spend some time in nature. You can go outside after dinner if you want to improve your digestion.

Once you have chosen how you want to get your time in nature, try to keep it consistent. It will help you choose a place that feels safe. Remember that the time you spend in nature is only helpful in relieving stress if you are able to embrace the experience in a relaxed way. To maximize the benefits you get from being outside, try as much as you can to stay present. Take deep breaths and be sure to pause when you need to, observe what is around you, and take in the experience.

Chapter 3:
Yoga Stretches to Help You Relax

A lot of research has been done to understand the way yoga helps in stress reduction. One way it helps in relaxation and stress relief is through the nervous system, particularly the autonomic nervous system and the way it responds to stress. Yoga conditions the nervous system to be able to respond better to emotional stress by building its endurance through physical stress. That's why any form of yoga, even the really demanding poses, can help you destress.

Think of it this way – if you could spend all your time in the most peaceful and quiet environment, then stress would not be a problem. Yoga makes that a reality by making your nervous system resilient. Both the vigorous and slower practices improve your nervous system's ability to find balance and deal with stress.

There's also growing evidence that yoga is one of the mind-body interventions. It lowers the inflammatory response which causes stress, aging, and disease in the body. At the same time, it also improves the tail-end genes known as telomeres, which can fray and shorten because of factors like poor nutrition, aging, chronic stress, and disease. Yoga lengthens and strengthens the telomeres which protect your genes from any damage.

A 10-Minute Routine

You don't have to enroll in a yoga class to benefit from yoga. With only 10 minutes a day, you can start experiencing the relaxation benefits of this practice and turn it into a habit. There are many yoga resources online that you can use to get you started, but here I'll provide you with a 10-minute routine that I've used for a long time and found helpful. Repeat it until the movements become natural, and until you're ready to shake things up. To do this routine, you only need yourself and probably a yoga mat.

Find a spot that you find comfortable and where you can be uninterrupted for 10 minutes. You can have a blanket or a cushion to provide you with support so that you're in a comfortable seated position. If you're feeling up to it, you can do the following routine outside.

Begin with mindfulness.

Focus on your breath so that you slow down your body and your brain and get in the moment. As you go into each yoga pose, remind yourself that the practice is about self-respect and self-care. Practice curiosity toward yourself if your thoughts start running all over the place. This will put you in the right headspace for your practice.

1. As you're seated, let your shoulders relax. Clench your stomach and extend your tailbone. The idea is to straighten your back and lengthen it from the top of your head. Breathe in for six seconds as you keep your stomach tight. Exhale and allow the stomach to relax completely. Repeat this a number of times until you start to get into a rhythm.

2. With your legs crossed, relax your feet. Let your pelvis be neutral and concentrate on your breathing. Sit for a minute and notice the sensations that are going through your body when you're unrushed, aware, and still.

3. Gently let your head fall forward into your chest and move it slowly into a full circle three times to the right and thrice to the left. This is called the neck roll. Invite the feeling of release, and then return to a neutral position.

4. Roll your shoulders in circular motions backward four times and then repeat the same movement forward. After doing the shoulder roll, inhale and

bring your hands over your head. Exhale while bringing your hands together at your chest.

5. Gently move onto your knees and hands, keeping your wrists directly below your shoulders and your knees aligned with your hips. You want your fingers to be facing forward with your palms on the floor. Evenly distribute your weight on your palms, center your head, and soften your gaze so that you're looking downward. Stay in this position for 30 seconds.

6. Breathe in as you drop your belly toward the floor. Raise your chest and chin so that you face the ceiling. Draw your shoulders away from the ears. Exhale as you pull your stomach inward and round your back. Release your head to face the floor. Repeat these movements up to five times slowly and in rhythm.

7. The next position is called the downward-facing dog. Tuck the toes under your feet and your palms on the floor. Lift your hips, extending your tailbone upward, forming an upside-down V. Push the heels back and down toward the floor. You don't have to touch the ground with your heels. Let your head drop and hold for a few seconds.

8. While standing, slowly move your hands toward the feet and let your shoulder and neck muscles relax. Release the weight of your head and

straighten your legs. Cross your forearms and press your heels into the floor while your tailbone faces the ceiling. Loosen your neck and hold for a few breaths before releasing your arms to be straight.

9. Get into the mountain pose – bend your knees and tuck your stomach then stand up. Extend the tailbone and breath in with your hands at chest level. Slowly lower your hands toward your feet and release your shoulders and neck. Keep your legs straight. If you struggle to keep your legs straight, you can bend your knees slightly and put one palm on the floor or on your cushion. Resist the urge to rest it on your knee. Raise the other hand over your head and try to keep your shoulders aligned by slightly twisting at your waist. Look up and hold for 20 seconds before repeating on the other side.

10. Finish your routine on the child's pose. Softly put your weight on your knees and extend your hands forward. Let your torso relax on your thighs. Leave some space between your knees but let your toes touch. If you can, let your buttocks touch the heels of your feet.

If these instructions don't work out for you, you can find hundreds of video guides for 10-minute yoga sessions on YouTube. Make sure to check them out.

Regulating Your Breath

Yoga has four main components including meditation, postures, breathing, and relaxation. These features are not exclusive but they complement one another. The most important one to master, if you want to reap the relaxation benefits of yoga, is how to breathe. In fact, breath is thought of as the guide in many aspects and types of yoga. In essence, yoga brings an increased awareness to breathing which gives you both psychological and physical benefits.

When we feel stressed, we often shorten or hold our breath. Sometimes we take in short, stilted breaths. Yoga will teach you to continue inhaling and exhaling calmly and deeply even in stressful situations, reducing the amount of stress you experience. Throughout the routine and as you move through the different poses, try and regulate your breath – that is the most transferable skill in yoga that you can bring into your daily life. Here are two breathing exercises you can do just before yoga, in your first two minutes.

1. Sit comfortably and keep your legs crossed and your eyes closed. Breathe in from your belly and move through your chest. Think of it as if you're filling your body with air up to your throat. Exhale through your throat, chest, and belly, and repeat five times.

2. Alternatively, sit in a kneeling position with the heels tucked beneath the hips. If you have knee problems, you can sit with your legs crossed for this one too. Put one hand over your heart and the other one on your belly – choose the hands as it comes naturally to you. Close your eyes and breath in and out to the mantra of *hold* on the inhale and *release* on the exhale. Repeat five times before opening your eyes.

As you keep practicing this yoga routine, some positions will get easier and you'll be able to integrate other yoga stretches. You will also begin to find it easier to combine breath with your body movement. Based on where you look, some trainers will ask you to inhale into a position, hold your breath, and exhale as you change. That gets easier with time so don't get discouraged if you're unable to do it from the get-go.

Practicing Yoga Anywhere

As it is, your 10 minutes of yoga can take place anywhere, not necessarily within the confines of your home. You can use the time you spend commuting, changing classes, or between events to practice. To make it easier for you, start small. The sequence I've provided is a good place to begin.

You may think of yoga as what happens in an hour-long class, but the few postures you do for 10 minutes have incredible benefits. Only make sure that you're practicing in a quiet place. If that's not a possibility, put on your headphones or play some calming music from YouTube.

Try to practice at the same time each day in the beginning so that you can work yoga into your daily routine, but do not give up if you forget to do your routine for a day. You can always go back to it.

Chapter 4:

HIIT Workout to Get Into Shape

Most of us agree that physical activity is healthy. Even so, research estimates that more than 20% of people all over the world do not get nearly enough physical activity every day. In the US alone, the number is placed at 80%. Imagine that.

Unless the work you do is physically demanding, having a dedicated fitness routine may be your best bet for staying active and healthy. However, the majority of us either don't have enough time or we feel like we don't have enough time, and that gets in the way of exercise. If that sounds like you, you may want to try HIIT (High-Intensity Interval Training). HIIT has been proven to provide similar health benefits to regular workouts, but in less time. It helps you reduce body fat, increase your metabolic activity, and lower your blood pressure.

HIIT is a broad term that is used to refer to any number of workouts involving a short period of intense exercise alternated with a short recovery period. One of its biggest advantages is that you get its maximal benefits to health in minimal time.

Generally speaking, you can do HIIT for up to 20 minutes, but the recommended time here is 10 minutes, so that you hit the sweet spot when it comes to time, challenging yourself just enough to get in shape, but not so much that it causes you to give up. Despite the fact that you work out for only 10 minutes, you get as many health benefits as you would if you worked out twice as much, doing moderate-intensity exercise.

The actual activity you do can vary from biking and sprinting to bodyweight exercises or jumping rope, but the idea is the same – you alternate an intense workout with short rest periods. For example, doing a HIIT workout with a stationary bike, you could cycle as fast as possible for 30 seconds, using the maximum possible resistance, and then take a minute of slow, easy cycling at low resistance, before exerting yourself again.

You repeat this cycle for 10 minutes and call it a day. Regardless of the way you implement the strategy, you should have high-intensity intervals with vigorous exercise that speeds up your heart rate before doing a low-intensity interval.

Benefits of HIIT Workouts

HIIT workouts can burn many calories in a short time. It's the perfect solution for burning a good amount of fat quickly. One study compared the number of calories burned during each HIIT session involving biking, running, and weight training.

Researchers found that people who exercised using HIIT burned 30% more calories than those who were doing other forms of exercise. The study had participants doing one HIIT repetition consisting of 20 seconds of maximum effort and 40 seconds of rest. This means that participants were really just exercising for a third of the time. The difference in the number of calories burned was because HIIT allows you to burn as many calories as you would in a longer workout session, but you spend less time exercising.

HIIT also raises your metabolic rate for hours even after the workout, which helps with weight management and weight loss. A number of research studies have demonstrated its ability to increase your metabolic rate up to five hours after a 10-minute exercise.

Some studies have found that it raises your metabolism after exercise way more than weight training or jogging. In fact, HIIT could shift your metabolism toward burning fat for energy instead of carbs. Consequently, this helps you lose fat.

One review, intending to find out how HIIT helps with fat loss, considered 13 experiments on 424 adults with obesity or who were overweight. The review found that both traditional moderate-intensity exercise and HIIT reduce waist circumference and body fat but HIIT reduces fat faster and with a shorter time commitment. Some researchers tout it as the most effective workout for people with obesity or overweight.

As if that's not enough, HIIT helps you gain muscle. It has been found to increase muscle mass in some people. However, the increase in muscle mass is majorly in the muscles you use the most, so it matters the kinds of exercises you do during your HIIT training. If you were less active before beginning HIIT, you're more likely to see more increases in muscle mass compared to someone who was pretty active.

Research looking at the effects of HIIT on relatively active people showed that the increases in muscle mass were lower. You may want to sprinkle your HIIT with weight training if your goal is to gain muscle mass and you were active before picking up HIIT.

Due to the nature of the workout, HIIT can improve your oxygen consumption. Oxygen consumption refers to your muscle's ability to utilize oxygen. People who have high endurance have high oxygen consumption. That's why, traditionally, endurance training is recommended if you want to up your oxygen consumption.

This would look like continuous cycling or running at a steady rate. However, you can get the same benefits with HIIT. One researcher looked at participants who did a 10-minute HIIT workout four days a week for a month and found their oxygen consumption increased by 9%. This improvement was identical to the oxygen consumption improvement in another study group involving participants who cycled continuously for 40 minutes every day, four days a week for a month.

The same researcher, trying to further their study, compared their findings from the HIIT participants to another group of people who exercised for eight weeks on stationary bikes. They found HIIT participants to have a higher increase in oxygen consumption.

Again, HIIT proved to be better in its results than a traditional 60-minute moderate-intensity exercise. The study participants who did HIIT also had an added benefit – they reported a reduced heart rate and blood pressure.

There's a huge body of research to support the fact that HIIT can lower blood pressure and heart rate in people with obesity and overweight, for whom high blood pressure is very common. One study looked at people doing HIIT for eight weeks on stationary bikes. They were found to have lower blood pressure compared to another group of adults who did endurance training. In this research, endurance training involved working out four days every week for 30 minutes a day. The HIIT group worked out only thrice per week for 10 minutes per day.

However, HIIT does not have such a huge impact on blood pressure for people with a normal BMI.

The final benefit of HIIT is its ability to lower blood sugar. HIIT programs that last less than 12 weeks have the ability to reduce blood sugar according to research from the University of Chicago. HIIT doesn't only lower blood sugar, it also betters insulin resistance compared to more traditional ways of exercising. This makes it a resource for people with a risk for type 2 diabetes.

Some experiments have specifically zoomed in on people with type 2 diabetes and found HIIT to be effective in helping them to manage the disease. In healthy people, HIIT may improve insulin resistance as well, better than traditional continuous exercise.

Getting Started With HIIT

While HIIT has so many health benefits, it also improves athletic performance in both aerobic and anaerobic activities. You don't have to be an aspiring athlete or weekend warrior to enjoy HIIT. It can make you more effective in day-to-day activities that require movement.

By setting aside only 10 minutes of your day, you get to improve your performance in other tasks. There are many ways you can make HIIT part of your daily routine, so it's not hard to get started. All you need to do to start is to pick an activity – this could be jumping rope, biking, running, or any other physical activity. From there, you can experiment using different exercises and recovery durations.

To make sure that you're much more likely to stick with your routine, make sure you pick an activity that you're familiar with. You want to remove as much resistance for yourself as possible. Be sure that you're able to perform the activity well and effectively, with the right form, at a lower intensity.

For example, do not jump head-on into sprinting if you haven't done any jogging in the recent past. Instead, start slowly and work your way up. If you struggle with joint pain, pick an activity that won't aggravate it. This could be low-impact modalities like swimming or cycling.

At the beginning stages of your workout sessions, take rest periods that are long enough. You can maintain the highest possible intensity for HIIT only if you're able to take rest periods that are longer or at least equal to your workout periods. Try and keep the workout periods less than 30 seconds in the beginning. Going longer than 30 seconds may make the session difficult to continue, because you'll struggle to sustain the intensity required for the workout to be HIIT.

HIIT is demanding especially when you pick higher-impact modalities. You also need to give yourself sufficient rest and recovery time, so pick times of the day to workout that can allow you enough rest for the rest of the day, and then workout again at the same time the next day so that your muscles have at least 23 hours of recovery time.

To get started, you can do your HIIT on a stationary bike. Pedal as hard as you can and as fast as possible for 25 seconds, then continue pedaling slowly and at an easy pace for up to three minutes or until you feel sufficiently rested. Repeat this cycle three more times.

If you prefer to run, begin by jogging for a minute to warm up. Then, sprint as fast as you can for 15 seconds. Jog or walk at a slow pace for up to two minutes and repeat the pattern until your 10 minutes are over.

You can also do HIIT using bodyweight exercises. For example, you can do squat jumps as quickly as you can for 25 seconds, then stand for a minute to rest. You repeat the jumps and rest intermittently for the whole 10-minute workout period.

Simply put, you can modify any type of exercise or routine to be HIIT based on your preferences. Make sure you experiment with different routines and timings to find an option that suits you best. You will find HIIT to be very efficient at burning calories and helping you stay in shape. It will also give you many of the health benefits discussed earlier.

Chapter 5:
Plan a Healthy Diet

There are many benefits to following a healthy diet, including strong bones, prevention of disease, boosted mood, and protection of the heart. Generally speaking, a healthy diet includes foods that are dense in nutrition. Your body needs food from all the major food groups, including whole grains, lean proteins, fruits, vegetables, and healthy fats.

Eating healthy is also about replacing the foods in your diet that contain added salts, trans fats, and sugar with options that are more nutritious. Admittedly, eating healthy can be a lot of work. No wonder many of us struggle at it, what with other things gunning for our attention. We end up sacrificing our health for everything else.

Thankfully, by sparing only 10 minutes a day, you can take back control of your eating habits, plan your diet, and set yourself up for eating healthy, even in the middle of a very busy day. Before discussing how, let's delve into all the ways you can take the time. How exactly does a healthy diet help you?

Why a Healthy Diet?

According to the CDC (Centers for Disease Control and Prevention), heart disease is one of the leading causes of death for adults in the US. The American Heart Association (AHA) says that nearly 50% of all adults in the US have one form or another of cardiovascular disease.

Hypertension or high blood pressure is a growing concern – it could cause a stroke, heart failure, or a heart attack. It's possible to prevent up to 80% of premature stroke and heart disease diagnoses by making simple lifestyle changes, such as physical activity and eating healthy.

If we choose the right foods to eat, it can lower our blood pressure and help us keep healthy hearts. The right dietary approaches can help you manage or stop hypertension. You have to eat whole grains, fruits, and vegetables in plenty, because the right dietary approaches include healthy foods only. Your dairy products need to be low-fat or fat-free. You also need to know the kind of protein you're consuming, whether that's from beans, nuts, poultry, or fish.

A healthy diet also requires that you limit your intake of trans fat and saturated fats, which means avoiding fatty meats and full-fat dairy products. It means you limit the foods and drinks you take that have high levels of added sugars, and you restrict your intake of sodium to less than 2300 milligrams a day — less if possible — and increase your consumption of calcium, magnesium, and potassium.

To top it all, you need foods that are high in fiber to keep your heart healthy. According to the AHA, foods that are high in dietary fiber are good for you. Fiber improves blood cholesterol and reduces the risk of type 2 diabetes, obesity, stroke, and heart disease.

Besides this, the medical community has recognized the link between heart illnesses and trans fats for a long time, which is why it's recommended to limit some types of fats to improve heart health. For example, reducing trans fats from your diet lowers the levels of LDL (Low-Density Lipoprotein) cholesterol.

LDL cholesterol is responsible for plaque collecting in your arteries, increasing the risk of stroke and heart attack. It also helps reduce your blood pressure, keeping your heart healthy. The majority of adults achieve this by lowering their salt intake to less than 1500 milligrams a day. Of course, this is not easy if you're not keen to read the label on your off-the-shelf foods. As it is, food manufacturers add salt to many processed foods, and you can find out the amount of salt in your food by just reading the label.

A healthy diet is also said to reduce the risk of developing cancer. You could consume foods that are high in antioxidants to help lower the risk of getting cancer. Antioxidants protect your cells from damage.

It's the presence of free radicals in your body that increases the risk of developing cancer. Antioxidants work by removing these free radicals, lowering the risk of the disease. There are many phytochemicals found in vegetables, fruits, legumes, and nuts which act as antioxidants, including lycopene, beta carotene, vitamin E, vitamin C, and vitamin A.

Conforming to the reports from the National Cancer Institute, animal and laboratory studies show a clear link between certain antioxidants and a low risk of free radical damage because of cancer. The evidence is stacked for eating foods high in antioxidants. These are foods like berries, carrots, dark, leafy greens, pumpkin, seeds, and nuts. This is particularly advisable for people with obesity, because having obesity may increase your risk of developing cancer.

A study conducted in 2014 found that a diet that's rich in fruits lowers the risk of developing cancers in the upper gastrointestinal tract. Researchers also found that a diet that's high in fiber, fruits, and vegetables lowers the risk of colorectal cancer, while a fiber-rich diet lowers the risk of liver cancer.

What you eat also affects how you feel – the healthier your diet, the better your mood. In 2016, researchers were looking into the relationship between mood and diet, and they found that diets that have a high glycemic load tend to trigger symptoms of fatigue and depression in people with obesity, who are otherwise healthy. A diet with a high glycemic load means it has a huge number of refined carbohydrates.

Things like white bread, biscuits, soft drinks, and cakes have a high glycemic load. Whole grains, fruits, and vegetables have a low glycemic load.

Recent research sheds light on how what you eat also affects your blood glucose levels, your git microbiome, and your immune activation, all of which affect how you feel. The researchers were looking to understand how a healthy diet helps us stay content. They found that such diets inevitably result in better mental health.

The opposite is also true – if you eat foods high in fat and processed carbohydrates over an extended period, you'll notice your mental health deteriorating.

Apparently, there's a need to further research the links between diet and mental health, but what is known at the moment suggests that we're better off eating healthy.

Finally, a healthy diet means better gut health. The colon is filled with naturally occurring bacteria that play an important role in digestion and metabolism. Some strains of bacteria, for example, are instrumental in the production of vitamins B and K, which benefit the colon. They help our body fight against harmful viruses and bacteria.

Having a diet that's high in fiber lowers the risk of gut inflammation. You need plenty of legumes, fruits, fibrous vegetables, and whole grains for this. They provide a combination of probiotics and prebiotics which help the good bacteria in your colon to thrive. Practically, this means favoring fermented foods as well for their probiotics – things like sauerkraut, kimchi, and yogurt. They improve many digestive issues including IBS symptoms.

10-Minutes a Day for Your Diet

There's so much to remember about eating healthy that it can become challenging, especially if you have other responsibilities to deal with. The trick to sustaining a healthy diet is to begin small and make tiny lifestyle changes on a regular basis. These can make a significant difference.

That's what this chapter is about.

You need to take only 10 minutes out of your day to think about what you're going to eat for the rest of the day. How you spend those 10 minutes will vary – it's supposed to vary as you become more present and more committed to eating a healthier diet.

Perhaps in the first month, your 10 minutes will go toward getting practical knowledge surrounding healthy eating. As time goes by, you can spend them journaling about how you feel after eating certain foods or your weight management journey. After you're well aware of your body's needs and reactions, you can spend these 10 minutes planning your meals for the rest of the day or even days.

Whatever the case, here are some practical things you can do with your 10 minutes.

• Pack your snacks

When you're hungry and in a hurry, it's easy to turn to things like chips, muffins, and biscuits. In fact, more than 35% of the average daily kilojoule intake for an adult in the US comes from high-sugar and high-fat discretionary foods. But if you're careful to pack your snacks in your bag earlier on, you can guarantee that you'll eat better.

Make sure your snacks focus on the core food groups – whole grains, nuts, vegetables, and fruits – your body will thank you for it. You can pack things like air-popped popcorn, raw vegetable sticks, unsalted nuts, a plain yogurt with berries, whole grain toast, or reduced-fat milk. Fresh seasonal fruit also makes for good snacks.

• Place your foods thoughtfully

How many times do you open your pantry or your fridge, looking for something to snack on but you're not really sure what you want? There's a solution for that – food nudging.

Research shows that when you put food in places that are easy to reach, you can nudge yourself to make better and healthier food choices. A review of scientific studies done in 2016 found that changing where you put your food positively influences your eating habits. Supermarkets already do this, with the thoughtfulness they give to where everything is placed. You can use the same principle at home.

Put your healthy food in spots that are easy to spot. You can begin by stocking up your fruit bowl and putting it on an accessible surface in the kitchen or dining table. The idea is to make it easy for you to grab a healthy snack at home or while you're on your way out.

Alternatively, you can chop up some raw vegetables and fruit and put them in transparent containers at an easy place to reach in the fridge. In the same vein, keep treats such as chocolate at the back of the cupboard so that they are out of your sight.

• Make a grocery list

How many times have you gotten into a shop to get bread and milk and come out with more groceries? A grocery list can always save you money and time at the supermarket. It can also help you stay committed to eating healthy.

A study conducted in the US found that people who use a checklist when shopping for groceries tend to have healthier weight management even when they're shopping in places with fewer healthier options. Keeping a list would counteract most of the marketing influences and techniques coming at you in the store.

At least one day each week, spend your 10 minutes planning out what your typical meals or snacks would look like. Group your foods by category and then make a list of all the fresh vegetables and fruits you need, so that you make only one trip to the store and save yourself the time you'd spend doubling back for missed items. Keep your list in a central place so that your family can make their additions as needed, and see how much healthier your grocery shopping will become.

If you can think of nothing else that's diet-related to spend your 10 minutes on, spend them preparing your breakfast.

Most mornings are a rush. We end up skipping breakfast or snacking on something unhealthy. Then we get into the habit of grabbing donuts or coffee on our way to work. So you can spend your 10 minutes portioning your cereal into a bowl and keeping it ready to take with you to work. You can spend them making a batch of fresh fruit and muesli, or you could whip up small frittatas to eat as you begin your day.

Preparing your own breakfast and taking your time with it also counts as self-care, and it will automatically put you in a better mood for the rest of the day. Not to mention the nutritious meal your body will be consuming.

Eating breakfast helps keep your glucose levels stable and regulates your appetite, which means that you're less likely to overeat for the rest of the day. Research has proven that people who skip breakfast end up having less nutritious diets and tend to be overweight. Just 10 minutes each day can sort your breakfast out and mean that you begin your day better.

Chapter 6:
Ground Yourself Through Meditation

Our world today is characterized by never-ending to-do lists, causing many of us to feel as though we can't keep up. Work deadlines take priority over your relationships, health, and family. Internal and external conflicts become the norm. Before you know it, you're always rushing somewhere to do something. You just never seem to stop.

And yet, there are some people who are able to manage their energy output well. They look like they've found their system; they're capable of balancing their responsibilities — going after their goals and taking some downtime. They come off as being centered, grounded, and calm. What is their secret? How can you be able to balance your children, career, health, and personal growth like them in a way that feels harmonious?

This is where meditation comes in.

Before jumping into it, here's some background. Not so long ago, the topic of 'energy' was thought of as 'woo-woo' language, reserved for New Agers and with no basis in reality. The idea of having any ability to wield energy to heal ourselves and others seemed too mysterious and delusional, because it's not something tangible or visible. But thanks to many therapeutic techniques, it's been acknowledged and accepted by more and more people who are starting to see the place of grounding techniques.

Science has also provided evidence that has added to this acceptance and evolution. Scientists agree that everything is made up of energy. It requires energy to run generators, turn lights on, or power anything. Yet, energy is not just applicable in the context of fueling your tank to get to work.

There's a reason we describe people who are especially jazzed up as 'full of energy.' When you're feeling depleted after a stressful day, we use language like 'feeling drained' or 'needing to recharge'. It's as though we recognize a truth on a subconscious level that we're unwilling to accept – we are made up of energy.

If you're made of energy, though, can there really be a shortage of energy inside of you?

I argue, there cannot. It's not your energy that's depleted at the end of a particularly stressful day. You're actually emotionally, mentally, or physically exhausted. Your tank may metaphorically be running dry, but it's not literally dry. What has changed is your emotions, mindset, or physical body. It's how you use your energy that affects these changes.

Energy is always shifting, moving, or transforming based on your intentions, the motives behind your actions, your environment, and the things you choose to focus on. Energy will attract the energy that's like itself. All you need to do is notice how you're responding to interactions with others, news, or conversations on social media, and you will see the transference of similar energy.

When the evening news hypes something, you end up feeling emotionally and mentally hyped. When people argue over their differences on social media, you end up feeling angry and annoyed, and you respond with your own behaviors stemming from anger which makes you feel even more annoyed. On and on it goes.

Meditation is about learning how to identify and then direct your energy so that you have more control over your emotional and mental states. In effect, this influences your actions at any and all moments.

Traditional meditation techniques, depending on the geographical area and type of practice, would begin with the foundational steps to work with air, fire, water, and earth. They believed that these elements also exist at an energetic level within us. They are what the universe is made up of, and they have different expressions and energies. As such, many meditative practices would be geared towards connecting with the elements on both the metaphysical and physical planes. The belief was that connecting with the natural world gives us greater levels of awareness and control, and improves our well-being.

While you may not move to the French Alps to become a monk, you can still reap the same benefits of grounding meditation. It helps to calm your nervous system. It reduces cortisol and improves vagal tone, which is linked to prosocial tendencies like increased creativity, kindness, generosity, and cooperation. It's an excellent way to deal with fear and anxiety. So if one of your goals is to become more confident, taking 10 minutes out of your day to meditate will get you there.

Adding Meditation to Your Daily Life

Meditating has been around for a long time. It's the center of many religions. Through meditative practices, you can free your mind from stress and anxiety. You become more mindful of your surroundings and your body, and it gets easier to figure out what's bothering you in good enough time to deal with it.

Yet, one of the difficulties people encounter when trying to integrate meditation into their daily lives is finding the time. You can take any 10 minutes off your day, but I suggest three things that you can use as cues to form the habit of meditation:

• When you feel like scrolling social media

Many of us are in the habit of mindlessly scrolling through social media, due to which we end up wasting time we could use on our goals. You can set yourself up to meditate as a response to the urge to scroll through Instagram or Twitter. Chances are, the inspiration you expect to find there is already in your brain, so taking a step back from social media to meditate will help you tap into it.

So the next time you feel like checking your newsfeed, how about taking those 10 minutes off to meditate?

• Just before going to bed

Alternatively, you can meditate for 10 minutes just before going to bed. It's an excellent option if you're struggling to make meditation into a habit. The cherry on top is that meditation also improves your sleeping patterns. Research has shown that meditating just before bed is like listening to calming music. They both help you to unwind the conscious brain and relax your body.

• During your commute

There are times when you feel stressed and it seems to be out of nowhere. Maybe you thought you were on top of your work responsibilities but then you forgot something. Or perhaps you got a stressful email before a meeting. If you're commuting, that's a good time to take your 10 minutes out for meditation. You can simply put your phone away and put your mind at ease.

A Meditation Technique

The next obstacle people have when trying to add meditation to their lifestyle, other than time, is know-how. You have set aside your 10 minutes for meditation, now what? Here's a technique that can help you get started.

1. Find a comfortable place to sit, as far away from distractions as possible. Close your eyes. Focus on your breathing and take slow, deep inhalations and exhalations.

2. Picture a white light coming from a source directly above you and see that energy coming into your body through your head. Imagine the energy moving through your spine, out through your feet into the earth.

3. Imagine, feel, or see any energy imbalances inside you getting moved into the earth to leave you feeling balanced. Then bring pure, reliable energy back into yourself through your feet and into your whole body.

4. Allow yourself to experience what you imagine this light to feel like in your body – that feeling

could be something like security, safety, permanence, reliability, or whatever you need at the moment. When you feel the sensation, affirm it in yourself. Remind yourself that you can access it anytime you need to.

5.   Open your eyes slowly and make a note of any of the things that come up in your mind, if at all, then proceed with your day.

Meditation is one of the quickest and simplest ways to ground yourself – bring yourself into a balanced, centered, and calm state. The best part of it is that you can do it anywhere and anytime by yourself, and as much as you need to. The more you meditate, the better you'll become at it, and the easier it will be to take back control of your emotional and mental states.

What to Expect When You Meditate

Admittedly, when they're just starting out, many people struggle. You hear questions like, 'What am I supposed to feel?' and 'How do I know it's working?'

Meditation requires patience, because at first, your mind may be the biggest obstacle. You may find yourself distracted by your thoughts every time you try to meditate. That is normal. Meditate anyway. When your thoughts try to get in the way, simply notice them without judgment, and bring your focus back to your breathing. If your hopes, to-do lists, and worries threaten to overwhelm you, acknowledge them and then let them go. With time, your ability to stay with the practice will increase and you'll begin having experiences that confirm that your meditation is working. Your sensations and thoughts will get less and less likely to disturb your meditation practice. With meditation, however, remember that the journey is the goal.

Even so, as you meditate, your concentration will improve. You will find it easier to give your full attention to one activity at the same time. This is because meditation makes us aware of our present moment without judgment, which makes us feel less stressed about the future.

You fully inhabit the here and now, and as that improves, so does your ability to focus on one single task efficiently. With time, your meditation will start to show in terms of psychological or physical changes. People may start to notice how much more present you are. That is proof that what you're doing is working. As a way to track your progress with meditation, watch out for things like:

- Better awareness
- Better relationships
- Natural mindfulness, and
- More ease during the actual practice

In the beginning, it is likely that meditation will feel a little odd. That's normal. Do not try to analyze or replicate any experience you have during meditation. Simply keep a natural, neutral, and objective awareness of what's happening in your mind. Eventually, you will loosen the restraints of self-centeredness and move toward a subtle kind of awareness. You will grow less self-conscious and experience an abiding and profound sense of peace. Isn't that what we all want?

Chapter 7:
Gain Clarity Through Journaling

Writing can be a powerful tool to understand and organize your mind. Our world today is uncomfortably loud. Although you may spend time with your friends and family, there's still incessant noise from social media and 24-hour news cycles that brings chaos and confusion to your mind. This is coming at a time when researchers are reporting the highest numbers of depression and anxiety cases stemming from things like financial instabilities, mass unemployment, and personal tragedies.

Journaling is the easiest way to gain clarity in your thinking. It allows you the space you need to structure your thoughts without the stress of publicizing your work. For only 10 minutes a day, you can get insight into the way your life is unfolding, grow your connection with yourself, and identify the areas you need to improve.

Journaling has changed the way I do things in my life; from connecting with others to planning my days. It has provided me with a platform to negotiate with myself on how to improve. My close friend, Cassie, says that she has experienced the same thing with journaling.

Cassie is an introvert who always found the world to be too loud and overwhelming. All through her life, she had been quiet to the point of being described as a mute child. She had to deal with a huge level of anxiety just to function normally. Cassie says that she always found solace in keeping a journal and writing down her thoughts.

Thankfully, she learned about journaling in her early teenage years and has kept the practice since. She says that among other benefits, journaling has helped her to know her thoughts and to know herself. On campus, when she had an anxious period coupled with depression, she tried counseling for the first time. She was given antidepressant drugs, which also helped, but she says it's journaling that really got her out of the woods.

Scientific Benefits of Journaling

Other than anecdotal evidence, there's a lot of scientific evidence backing the importance of journaling. Keeping a journal keeps your thoughts and ideas organized. Our thoughts are like the wild west or a chaotic nightmare when the mind is left unsupervised. They come as they wish and roam where they want. Just try to think about a specific thing for only three minutes, and you'll see what I mean.

Journaling helps to free up your mind. It removes you from the thinking loop you're stuck on. Through journaling, you limit the data that appears to be important at the moment, by saving the important details on paper or on your computer.

Research has also shown that journaling keeps you responsible. Researchers from Cambridge University considered 50 people in alcoholism recovery. 90% of the people who kept a journal were able to stay sober over a period of three years compared to the 43% of those who did not keep a journal of their recovery journey.

All the respondents who kept a journal were required to just put a note in each entry that they were still sober at the end of the day – nothing much; no fanfare. And even that worked to keep them on track with their decision to stay sober. You can use the same idea for any habit you want to keep up.

Take John, for example. John wanted to become a writer, so he wrote that down. Every day, he resolved to publish a post on his blog. For three months, he promised himself that he would write a paragraph no matter what. He would then note the achievement in his journal at the end of the day. After having achieved and surpassed his goal at the end of the quarter, John says that it was journaling that kept him accountable. It brought him clarity because he had to log his desires and progress, ready to review after every week. His attention was kept on what he truly wanted.

Journaling also helps to regulate anxiety. It helps you calm down or get excited about the things that matter. You get to leave your worrisome thoughts on paper and remind yourself of the important ones, building momentum toward the tasks you need to do. Writing things down keeps your stress in check. It keeps you mindful of your focus and allows you to continue living without the sense of impending doom that anxiety brings. It shows you your next step and reminds you what to do without having to keep that thought in your mind.

When you have journaled for a while, you can use your journal to discover the patterns in your life. Writing down your thoughts, feelings, and fears will show you your tendencies. You may find that there are certain events you react to in a certain way. You may identify reactions you would rather not repeat. It's easier to notice these patterns in a journal than when you're trying to rely on your memory alone, and finding patterns allows you to correct or cherish them.

More than anything else, journaling helps you process your emotions. When you're in the middle of an emotional response, it can be impossible to focus on other things. Journaling allows you to know what emotions are responsible for the response, so that you can decide how better to respond in the long term.

Imagine you were just about to attend your kid's play. You were excited about it and you were looking forward to it, but then you got informed that your friend was issued a divorce by his wife. At that moment, your emotions are spilling. You identify with them so much they appear to define you. Even if you attend the play, you would still be thinking about your friend's troubles.

Even if your kid's play is significant to the whole country in this situation, would you be able to fully focus?

Journaling helps you increase your chances of paying attention. It allows you to lay aside the busyness, especially after hearing troubling news so that you can control your emotions and calm down. It allows you to process your emotions so that they're not lingering in your head all the time.

How to Journal

There are many ways to journal. Pick one that works for you and stick with it. You can also try out a combination of different styles, just as long as you spare 10 minutes out of your day to journal. You can journal by brainstorming or making lists. If you're the kind of person who loves to plan, making lists can help you to keep your sanity.

Make that list even if you don't think you'll see it through. Use it as a way to relieve stress.

Within those 10 minutes, write all the mindless thoughts and tasks that are clogging up your brain. It will help you sleep at night, just knowing that those thoughts have been acknowledged and recorded and you no longer have to remember them.

Each day, make a list of as many things as you can identify to do. Don't make them mandatory. The point of journaling by list-making is a place to release. If you make the tasks a must, you'll only guarantee that you feel guilty if you don't achieve them. Make lists for everything whether it's blog post ideas, the kinds of books you want to read, popular travel destinations, or where you want to be at the end of the year. It will stop your brain from going into overdrive.

Alternatively, you can journal through expressive or reflective writing. When you set aside your 10 minutes, write exactly what comes to your mind at that time without editing yourself. There should be no pressure on yourself to write poetically or nicely. You'll find the process strangely cathartic.

Try expressing every one of your anxieties, feelings, concerns, and thoughts, and see where that takes you. You are, in a sense, filling the paper with the breathings and breakings of your heart, as one philosopher put it.

There's no limit to the number of things to write about, but if you start to feel stuck, you can use journal prompts to help you get started.

As you sort through the litter in your head that you don't want to be exposed to the public, you'll notice that you feel better and you think better. Expressive writing is a form of self-care. It's about creating a space where you can be yourself and no one else. You don't have to perform, unlike other avenues like blog posts and social media posts, where you have to juggle other people's expectations. Here, you're completely alone with your innermost self.

If all else fails, you can also do stream-of-consciousness writing. It's similar to expressive writing, but it's ultimately carefree. Rather than thinking a little bit about what you want to write or which area of your life you'll explore next, you just let the words flow as they will. It may sound strange and may take some getting used to, but it's incredibly powerful.

By allowing your thoughts and words to just leap onto the page, you leave yourself free to just be, and create a calmer mind. The rule of thumb is not to second guess your thoughts. Just write what you see, feel, or think at the moment. Do not reread it. Just let the words come. Inevitably, you'll experience a sense of relief and your mind will feel lighter.

Make it a Routine

Like with the other habits in this book, you don't have to be writing for two hours every day to reap the benefits of journaling. Only set aside a definitive 10 minutes every day specifically to journal. Calendar it if you have to, or make it an item on your to-do list.

Even if you don't feel like it, journal about how you don't really want to journal. You'll find in a short while that the process becomes addictive. Then you'll want to do it more. Do not burden yourself with thoughts or ideas about how your journal should look like. The important thing is to do the actual journaling. The hows tend to vary from person to person and from day to day. Start however comes easily to you.

Journaling is about clearing your mind so that you live better. There are no requirements. You're the one who sets the rules. Your journal should serve you, so make it yours.

Chapter 8:
Read a Book to Expand Your Ideas

According to Oscar Wilde,
"It is what you read when you don't have to,
that determines what you'll be when you can't help it."

As it turns out, philosophers like Marcus Aurelius agree. No matter where you look, the most successful people in the world are people who spare time to read, study, and learn way beyond their school years. As a result, they become better leaders, innovators, and thinkers. With infinite knowledge at our disposal from books and the internet, there are way so many works out there to read, almost a little too much.

You can all agree that reading itself is an education. It teaches you nearly everything and anything you want to know. There are books on every topic that you can think about. Not only that, but reading also improves your spelling, grammar, and writing. It teaches you new words and more importantly, new ways to connect old ideas. Reading is the rawest way to learn.

To me, it's many things. It's a form of mindfulness, helping my mind escape my reality for a short period. It's a way to educate myself. It's a hobby and a source of peace. It has become a true passion of mine. But it wasn't always like that.

Reading Educates You

In many ways, there's a subjective aspect to reading. Some people like fiction while others enjoy non-fiction. Some people prefer children's books and others like science-based books. The topics you can read are truly endless. There's something for everyone. Whichever the case, reading will give you education.

When I started my 10-minute reading routine, I was barely testing the waters. I just wanted to develop a love for reading, but I read whatever I found as fast as I could. Then, as soon as I was done, I jumped onto the next book. I've always loved factual books, so I read some of those. I ventured into diet and science books to understand the human body and how different foods behave in the body.

After reading religiously for a while, often extending way beyond my 10 minutes, I came to the conclusion that I was not retaining as much information as I wanted. Of course, I knew I couldn't possibly remember everything I read, but I didn't like the fact that facts were passing my mind without sinking in and affecting how I was living. I found this frustrating because I also wanted to remember the information I read. My frustration continued as I kept extending the time I took to read, and often, I found myself rereading books so that I could gather the information I missed the first time around. I've been known to read books three times over.

Eventually, it seemed like I was just wasting my time, so I set out to find a solution. That's when I went back to the heart of taking on 10 minutes a day to read. I realized that the extra time I was adding was not helping me as much as I was hoping. It was only stealing from other things I needed to do and amplifying the pressure I was feeling to read fast and read a lot. I re-dedicated myself to the idea of reading for only 10 minutes a day and guess what, how I remembered the information I read changed. I retained more.

For the average reader, just 10 minutes of reading, no less, no more, averages to about 4 pages depending on the book they're reading. From a glance, it doesn't look like much, but if you've ever had to reread books, or if you struggle even to get started, there's no more productive way to read.

When I went back to reading for only 10 minutes a day, the proverbial ducks started falling in the row. Even though I was spending less time reading and taking longer to complete a book. I was understanding more of what I was reading. The four pages I read each morning could be digested in my mind throughout the day and somehow, they were put into practice.

I found that with reading hour after hour, page after page, with thousands of facts and words entering your mind, it's difficult to stay open to new connections to form between what you just read and what you knew before. When you read about four pages, you can nearly envision them all through the day. You rarely miss out on bits of information. In only 10 minutes, reading becomes true education.

Tips For Reading Every Day

Making reading a part of your daily habits can also mean pre-determining the time and content you set aside to read. As a rule of thumb, alternate between genres. That's one of the simplest ways to keep the flow of reading. Choose fiction when you need something entertaining. Go for non-fiction books when you're trying to learn something or master a new skill. Make sure that you have the book with you during your designated 10-minute reading period.

If you decide that you'll be reading at lunchtime, make sure you have your book with you. If you are to read before bedtime or after waking up, keep the book you're reading by your bedside. That way, you reduce the resistance when the time to read comes. If you can, have a physical copy rather than reading on your phone to avoid distractions.

Finally, make sure that you have your next book ready when you're almost finishing your current read. Once a fortnight, for example, take a trip to the bookstore and choose some books that interest you. It will be easier to keep to your reading schedule when you know you will not get stuck wondering what to read next.

Choosing Your Next Read

In the age of consumerism, you can get stuck consuming books like we consume many other things. The chances are that you can order books in bulk on Amazon, have an assortment of publication memberships, and need to catch up on some blogs that you like. How do you decide what to read and what to leave out? As someone who knows how it feels to sometimes pick up the wrong book and get demotivated by it, I've found some guidelines that can help you pick what to read next:

1. Read books by your favorite author

If you catch yourself struggling to decide what to read next, the easiest thing is to just pick a title from your favorite author. If you've liked and completed their works in the past, chances are you will like the next ones too.

2. Create a reading list

Every time you come across a book that interests you, add it to your list. Then, when it is time to decide on your next read, pick from the list the title that makes you most curious, accounting for your level of busyness, mood, and the specific period of your life. Try to pick a book that resonates with your natural needs, it will be easier to read.

3. Don't shop in bulk

This probably goes against your intuition, but the thing is, books have the ability to attract us with their exciting summaries, fancy covers, and compatibility with current learning needs and feelings. Buying books in bulk makes you think you will read one after the other, but by the time you have finished the first two, chances are the rest will not appeal to you – either they're not relevant to your situation anymore, or you don't feel like reading them.

4. Drop a book if it's not speaking to you

It will happen that sometimes you will pick up a book, get past some pages and then find that you're no longer interested in the book. You can't really focus or understand it. Do not continue out of a sense of duty. Feel free to quit and spend your 10 minutes on something you're more interested in.

5. Don't make it about numbers

A drawback of having a reading list is that it can demotivate you because you'll have so many options that you'll feel stuck. A list can make reading feel like something to tick off a dry list. Do not let it get there. Remind yourself that reading is an end in itself. It's not about the quantity of books, but the quality of learning. It will be easier to make reading into a new habit if it's fun. Lower your expectations for the number of books you read in a year, for example. It will take the weight off your shoulders and allow you to enjoy the benefits of reading rather than making it a boring chore.

Be patient enough to find your own pace and rhythm. Remember that it's about quality, not quantity. Pick the best books you can find, books that resonate with you so you can have enjoyable and fulfilling reading sessions.

Chapter 9:
Declutter Your Space to Gain Focus

Ever looked at those neat, tidy shelves in home décor blogs and felt a tinge of jealousy? Well-organized and minimalist space can be beautiful, but is minimalism for everyone?

Some research suggests that just by decluttering, you can positively influence your mental health to a great extent. Decluttering does as much good for your well-being as it does for your physical space. The thing is, that feeling you get when you see a tidy space is not just in your head. Having extra stuff can be stressful. If the constant number of things you have to pick up as you move around your house leaves you feeling anxious, it may be a sign that you need to declutter.

Objects have the power to leave us anxious. One researcher working with couples asked them to give a tour of their home. The findings revealed that women who used more words describing disorganization or clutter in their homes were also having higher levels of the stress hormone, cortisol. Conversely, those who saw their homes as being restful or who described the beauty in their outdoor spaces were less stressed and reported fewer feelings of sadness throughout the day.

This is because clutter takes away from our well-being. It makes it hard for us to focus.

Just think about it: how does it feel when you have a lot of things lying around on your work desk? You'll probably notice that it makes work seem harder than it actually is. A cluttered environment makes your brain less effective at processing information and makes you more prone to frustration. In other words, taking only 10 minutes a day to organize your space can save you time and energy and allow you to work more efficiently.

There's an old saying that goes, *'Show me your room, and I will tell you about your life.'*

The idea of the saying is that your space represents your intimate self and your identity. Some people think this saying has to do with the things inside your room and how they represent your personality, and that's part of it. The other part of is that your physical space mimics your mental space. That's why you feel better every time you clean up your room – there is a direct correlation.

About three years ago, Cynthia, a 25-year-old woman, had to re-explore the relationship between her room and her headspace. She had just quit her job to transition to entrepreneurship, and things were not picking up as fast as she had hoped. In three months, she had made only $150 in profits, and she was starting to fear that she made the wrong move.

She says that at some point, she became so unorganized that she lost her will. She was discouraged at not being able to save and barely making enough to pay her bills. Her savings were getting depleted fast and that was taking a toll on her. After observing her behavior for a week, her friend couldn't take it anymore. Gently, Cynthia's friend called her out, asking her to only clean up one aspect of her unorganized room a day.

Cynthia says she resisted it at first, and then just to keep the peace, she started by picking up some dirty laundry and putting it where it was supposed to be. The next day, she made her bed. After a week, she realized, in her own words, 'It's basic, but it works.'

Cleaning up her room made Cynthia feel better. It minimized the times she experienced sudden feelings of isolation and despair. It gave her a sense of control. Research shows that decluttering is an effective tool for doing just that. According to a study done at the University of Connecticut, removing clutter lessens the tension brought by messiness, but also leaves you feeling more self-assured and less apprehensive.

Other research also shows that the tendency to hoard can keep you up at night. Imagine that! A third of adults all over the world are dealing with sleep problems. While for a long time, experts have discussed the link between mental health conditions like anxiety and depression with insomnia, there's an emerging link in research – hoarding.

Between 2-6% of the US population is dealing with hoarding disorder, which extends beyond the tendency to accumulate unnecessary stuff. You're diagnosed with hoarding disorder when clutter gets so debilitating that your space is unusable and unsafe. One of the connections between hoarding and sleep is that without adequate sleep, you struggle to make decisions – including decisions to discard stuff.

For the other majority of people who don't suffer from hoarding disorder, simply having too much stuff also affects them. Consider the fact that having fewer things means having fewer choices to make all through the day. That translates to more willpower to spend trying to make the right choices.

What You Gain From Decluttering

Decluttering boosts creativity. It allows your mind to wander as you reorganize and think through your choices and possessions, which is relaxing. Researchers have noted that combining the physical activity of decluttering and the creativity it fosters leaves you feeling successful and accomplished. Not only that, but decluttering improves your focus.

If you ever find yourself struggling to focus, deal with the untidiness and clutter around you. It will make it easier for you to concentrate better when everything is where it's supposed to be. Your mind learns to stay on track to finish activities when it feels organized.

The study by Connecticut University also found that as people declutter, they're able to solve problems and finish tasks according to plan because they have a clear mind of what needs to be done. Decluttering sets productivity. The physical triumphs of decluttering give you vitality, and you can use that increased energy to tick off other tasks from your to-do list. The icing on the cake is that decluttering will make you less anxious and leave you feeling calmer.

How to Declutter

Thankfully, you don't need to remove all your clutter in one sitting. You can simply set aside 10 minutes of your day to declutter and organize just one part of your home, and do the other the next day. Since we have different needs, there's no simple method to use for decluttering, just principles that cut across the board. Regardless of how or when you organize and declutter, you allow your mind to rest.

• Declutter in stages

The first principle to observe, especially if you really have a huge pile of the clutter lying around your house, is to do it in stages. You can use the first week of your decluttering journey to make a checklist. Each day, for 10 minutes alone, make a list of the things that you would want to change, get rid of, or reorganize. Zoom in on each room individually and make the list as localized as possible. After that, take 10 minutes each day to complete one decluttering act, whether that's cleaning up one cabinet or taking out the trash.

• Sort through as you declutter

To avoid making more clutter, when you encounter a problem, solve it before moving to the next. For example, if you find an item, determine whether to put it away at a designated storage space, or to throw it away. Put the items together that are to be mended or fixed, and throw away the trash. Donate what needs to be donated when it comes up.

If you don't have a lot of stuff, you can easily declutter your house in one month by sparing only 10 minutes each day. Be sure to give yourself some buffer time though, in case you find your work cut out for you.

Avoid pulling out all your stuff without a plan for sorting through it. Without a plan, you'll end up just wasting your time. Consider beginning with a space with the least amount of clutter, so that you get it done quickly and feel like you're making progress early. It will motivate you.

Chapter 10:
Do a Brain Dump to Boost Creativity

By sparing only 10 minutes off your day, you can pull out a pen and paper to create a brain dump list that helps you release some mental pressure whenever your mind starts taking you in circles. Sometimes, your brain is a mess. You may be stressed, worried, anxious, or bursting with such random thoughts and ideas that you find it hard to focus. The inability to focus gets so frustrating, creating more stress. I find that when my brain is particularly haggard and restless, I start to fall out of my healthy habits and routines. The way to fix that feeling of being overwhelmed is to use the brain dump.

A brain dump refers to the act of dumping out all the contents of your mind onto a blank page the way one might dump the contents of a purse onto a table. Through a brain dump, you spill out your nagging thoughts, stressors, mental clutter, and every other annoyance to leave yourself ready to explore. You simply open up a valve in your mind and leave your thoughts to flow through your hand onto a piece of paper.

It's a bit like journaling, except in this case, you write until you feel that the pressure inside you has calmed. With a brain dump, you list all your anxieties and problems as a way to feel better.

Why a Brain Dump?

You may be wondering how exactly that helps. A brain dump is effective because it allows you to capture the abstract thoughts clogging up your mind. Every time you're stressed and overthinking, you have many thoughts going through your head and nothing to capture them. You may notice a nagging worry in your mind for a moment before it recedes to give way to a different thought, and then another one. Eventually, the first nagging thought swings by again, and the process continues like a loop until you pin down your thoughts.

Trying to capture your thoughts outside of writing (or venting) in a brain dump is like trying to catch smoke using your hands.

As you do a brain dump, you get to nail down your thoughts in absolutes, and once something is written down, it can't leave. It cannot begin another cycle in your brain to haunt you again – it stays right there where you wrote it. So you get a chance to work through those thoughts one by one, and you stop chasing distractions or half-formed ideas. You capture them in the form of the written word, achieving mental clarity and self-awareness. In simple terms, a brain dump helps you to:

- remember everything you need to do each day,

- organize your thoughts,

- concentrate better, and

- clear up your headspace, making space for creativity and learning.

One study conducted in 2021 found that students who participated in a brain dump activity had a lower intrinsic cognitive load. They also found it eas10ier to remember the things they studied compared to their counterparts. Another group of researchers was interested in finding out why a brain dump works to improve your mood, while only journaling about negative feelings left you feeling worse.

They found that the difference lies in what you do after the brain dump. To experience the best results, you have to be willing to make actionable conclusions from what you find in your brain-dumping exercise.

When Do You Do a Brain Dump?

You can do a brain dump at the beginning of the day if you're concerned about improving your productivity and focus. At the start of your day, you take out your brain-dumping notebook, set aside 10 minutes, and begin writing with no particular direction in mind. There are no rules. All you need to do is write your thoughts about the things you need to do for the day, what excites you, what thoughts hold you back, or the worries that are still lingering in your mind. This helps you organize your thoughts and helps you determine what's important for the day and what can wait till the next day.

You can also do a brain dump after you've learned a new skill or acquired new information. Doing a brain dump at this point can help you with recalling and revising the information later on. In educational research, this type of brain dumping is called retrieval practice.

For example, after reading a book on a subject you've been wanting to learn, you can simply write freestyle about everything you've absorbed. Some people find it better to create an organized list of the same information. Others separate it into different quadrants or categories. Whatever the case, the brain dump can help you with future recall.

You can even do it at work. Any time you come across a lot of new information, try to remember it by dumping it on a piece of paper. We learn in small bits, which is what makes this brain-dumping technique effective.

In case you don't learn any new information in your day, you can go for a gratitude brain dump. In this case, you write down every thought that has to do with things you're grateful for. Instead of writing about the negative experiences, you focus on the positive aspects of your life. Just set your timer for 10 minutes, and write down as many things as you can that you're grateful for.

You can make a list or write freehand. To get the most out of this brain dump, stay mindful. Pay attention to your feelings once you complete it, and keep the positive feeling you get with you as you go about the rest of the day.

Untangle Your Brain

How exactly do you go about doing the brain dump? On a piece of paper, begin anywhere and don't stop until you're either out of things to say, or you've exhausted eight minutes. Write down your list of weekend errands, your grocery list, or your plans to replant a container plant.

Nothing is exempt. As long as it comes to your mind, however weird or out of the ordinary it seems, write it. Your brain dump doesn't have to be about a specific topic; if it bugs you, it deserves to go there.

After you've finished writing, use the remaining two minutes to figure out your next step for just one thing that's bothering you. You can pick the thing that's stressing you out the most, or any item off your list that you like, as long as you pick one and make an actionable plan to deal with it. Sometimes, the issue you identify is something out of your control, so you can't plan around it. In such cases, let it go. Resolve to give up obsessing over what's not yours to control.

Do a brain dump every day to avoid feeling overwhelmed by too much brain activity. It's an effective way to relax your mind. Think of it like regular maintenance for your brain.

10-MINUTES A DAY FOR YOUR BUSINESS

The most successful businesses in the world are run by entrepreneurs who have the right set of habits to help them excel and thrive in the long term in the marketplace. A lot of how we behave comes from our daily habits, and this is true in business as well. Our habits determine our potential to shine at work. They're undeniably powerful in governing every aspect of our lives from the way we think, how we feel, how we act, and how we live our life. They have a massive impact on our potential to do well as businesspeople. Any business owner committed to doing well in their line of work needs to make sure they're cultivating the right habits.

Compared to other aspects of life, our business life is more prone to damage by our bad habits. Bad habits in the business world can destroy your reputation and kill any chances for success. Conversely, good habits, applied persistently, ultimately bring out a great success.

Considering the fact that out of every 10 businesses, eight of them fail in the first two years of being set up, and that only about 4%

of businesses hit the 10-year mark, the habits you employ can make or break you.

This section of the book has four habits that you can build in 10 minutes a day to make you a better business person. The list is not subjective – it's based on empirical data from the most successful entrepreneurs in the world.

The best entrepreneurs are motivated. They can keep going no matter what. They are problem solvers, goal-oriented, and adaptable. Each chapter will deal with one of these four qualities to help you make them into habits. If you focus on building these habits, long-term success for you is guaranteed.

However, do not expect overnight success. As I mentioned in the earlier chapters, there's no such thing as an overnight success. It will take some time, but as long as you are persistent, success will surely come.

Chapter 11:
Listen to Podcasts to Stay Motivated

Why Motivation Matters

Entrepreneurs are known for their commitment and tenacity. They're known for their ability to stay long hours, hold on to lofty ideals, and keep the hope of success burning. They're hard workers whose passion drives them toward a project and keeps them going until they make their mark. They have a peculiar knack for being able to convince people to see the value of their ideas. A key factor in keeping this kind of creativity, drive, and energy is motivation. Motivation is foundational to your ultimate success as an entrepreneur.

Motivation is the reason behind your actions. It's the thing that compels you to keep going and keep working. It gives you clarity and hope when circumstances are discouraging and tough. It's fundamental in your decision to start a business and to keep it going. It's also important to the people you work with or the people who work for you.

As a business person, you need to be able to help others tap into their own motivation and sustain it as you work together in business. You need to motivate other people to buy into your vision. Whether that looks like convincing an investment group to give you the startup funding you need, or it's about motivating your employees in the early days, you need to master this art.

Motivation keeps you on the same page about the mission of your business and gives you the fuel to continue working toward it.

Stay Inspired

Considering that there are many difficulties involved in building and running a business, motivation keeps you going, and getting into the habit of listening to podcasts can sustain that inspiration. The idea here is to find a podcast or podcasts that inspire you every day, and then use them to keep all your pistons firing at full steam.

For most of us, it helps to hear from someone who has already ventured into the places we long to go to, so that we model after them. You can listen to podcasts from the people you admire and the people you'd like to become. It will help you stay focused on your goals. You can listen to them talk about their journey, for example, every morning before you begin your day so that you keep your focus straight and sharp.

In truth, the most successful and the most famous people in the business world have failed at some point in their life. You can pick a podcast that reminds you of this, so that when you meet challenges in your own business journey, you stay inspired. Their stories will help you keep your dream alive in your mind. They provide a daily source of inspiration and proof that success is possible, despite momentary failure.

If that's not your cup of tea, you can pick podcasts that help you learn new business skills, useful business tips, and the latest news on what's happening in the business industry.

Podcasts are an excellent way for you to invest in yourself. You can learn about history, the arts, real estate investing, fashion, finance, and so much more by spending only 10 minutes of your day listening to a podcast. They allow you to get more educated and involved in your areas of interest. They make learning and developing entrepreneurial skills very easy.

The icing on the proverbial cake is that listening to podcasts will make you a better listener. Podcasts help us practice the simple act of listening, because that's all they're about. They allow you to get involved with what you're listening to by prompting you to pay attention and use your imagination to create pictures of what you're hearing. And being a good listener is as important as being a good speaker.

Essentially, podcasts engage different parts of your brain. They encourage you to listen actively, especially if they're on topics you feel about deeply. They're more than background sounds. They're the perfect medium for you to not just get entertained and involved, but to get inspired, all of which can boost your mental health.

In 2016, a study carried out at UC Berkeley came to the conclusion that listening to narrative stories, like in podcasts, excites different parts of the brain. The result is a release of feel-good hormones or endorphins, which boost your mood. A different study looked at people's brains while they were listening to a podcast they enjoyed. Researchers found that podcasts have the ability to stimulate more intense mental imagery than watching. Because podcasts are majorly audio, it forces you to build your imagination, which eventually makes you a better business person.

Getting Started

If there's one thing the internet is littered with is business advice. There are thousands of videos, podcasts, and online content claiming to know how best to run a business. One can see how it would be hard to know where to start choosing the right podcasts. Undeniably, this is the golden age of podcasts.

Going by data from Podcasthosting.org, 50% of all homes in the US listen to podcasts. 55% of the general population have interacted with at least one podcast every month, and 24% are committed to listening to a podcast every week. Since the medium has exploded in the last couple of years, it's possible that numbers will go even higher. As of 2020, there were more than a million podcasts and over 30 million episodes on different platforms, ready to stream into your ears.

Additionally, podcasts come in every style, format, and genre. You can find shows that are so highly produced that they sound like popular radio programs. There are conversational podcasts that feel like you're eavesdropping on a very private conversation. You can even find fictional shows which resemble old radio dramas.

For someone who's looking to grow their business, or to just get some daily motivation, how do you separate the filler content from the actionable and authentic ideas? How do you pick what works for you out of the seemingly good business podcasts all begging to be listened to? How do you avoid spending all your 10 minutes trying to choose a podcast to listen to every day so that you never get any listening done?

As a precursor to choosing a podcast to listen to, I suggest connecting to your business and life goals. Every business owner or entrepreneur is different, and so our motivation factors are different. Even so, there are things that are similar among entrepreneurs in terms of where they get inspiration and motivation. I've found that those factors can be grouped into four major categories:

· More freedom

Some people are driven toward entrepreneurship because they want to be their own boss. They no longer want to keep reporting or deferring to a certain structure. Or perhaps they just want the freedom to set their own hours. Entrepreneurship gives them that flexibility and freedom to decide how their careers unfold.

· More income

Some business people are driven by the thought of creating their own wealth. They turn to entrepreneurship as a way to get that. They want the opportunity to be able to make as much as possible by selling their products or skills. They figure that a business gives them the surest bet to increase their wealth over time.

· More influence

In some cases, when some people are working for a company as an employee, they disapprove of the direction the company is taking, and they choose to turn to entre-preneurship, so that they can have a hand in the way the business grows. They want more influence over the development of a product, the customer base, or the marketing. And entrepreneurship offers them this opportunity. This is a significant motivator for people who want to have a lasting impact or a legacy in a specific industry.

• Creativity and control

In other cases, entrepreneurs are driven by the need to express their creativity. They have ideas they want to share with the world that they believe would make people's lives better. and they want control over its execution. This could look like wanting to maintain creative control over the business processes and product development.

In which of these general categories do you fall?

If you can identify your greatest motivators for being an entrepreneur, you can commit to consuming content that taps into and enhances that. While at it, connect to your general goals for the business. What are you hoping to achieve in five years, for example? What skills do you need to get there? What are you currently trying to learn?

The idea here is to begin with you, so that you choose content that aligns with your values and goals and that helps you to move forward in business. You don't want to keep consuming content that doesn't immediately apply to your daily life.

Once you're connected to where you are in terms of your goals and your motivations, pick the kind of app you would love to stream from. There are many options to work from, based on whether you have an Android or iPhone. Pick your app and begin exploring.

Most of the apps have a selection of podcasts they suggest to you. You can look at that list and see if there's anything that stands out to you. You'll get many choices from the selections of suggested podcasts, whether your app of choice calls them trending, noteworthy, new, popular, or featured. Choose the ones that resonate with you and your goals. You can also look for podcasts by topic.

As you start listening to podcasts, you'll find that there are some of them that lend themselves to 'binge listening' and others that need you to space out your time. The temptation will probably be to spend more than 10 minutes listening to the podcast, especially if you find one that's really engaging.

Resist that urge. Remember that the goal is to make listening into a habit and to let it motivate you to do your daily tasks, not allow them to take up the tasks that make up your daily life. Once you feel sufficiently motivated, turn the podcast off and get working. Your business will thank you for it.

Chapter 12:
Solve Puzzles to Learn Problem-Solving

Some things wear out and then break over time. Others are flawed from the beginning. As a business person, you have to deal with many things, processes, interactions, and activities that are broken or simply aren't working as they should. Problem-solving provides you a mechanism to identify these things, figure out what is making them fail, and then determine how you're going to fix them.

That's what problem-solving is, in business – fixing the broken.

By definition, problem-solving is setting up processes that remove or reduce obstacles that are standing in the way of you or others achieving a strategic or operational business goal. As you do business, a problem is a situation that separates your desired outcome from the actual outcome. To solve the problem is to bridge that gap.

I've found that sometimes, a true problem doesn't always have an immediate and obvious solution, which is why every entrepreneur needs to grow their problem-solving muscles.

To adequately solve a problem, you need to be able to identify and define it. Then, you need the ability to prioritize so that you can deal with one business problem first, based on its size, urgency, and impact. That demands an ability to dig to the root cause and then come up with a number of possible solutions.

You also need to be able to evaluate those solutions so that you can choose which one will work best, and then you plan and put the solution into action. Whether it's conscious or not, every business person is always doing a level of problem-solving. They're working to resolve a conflict between two team members, trying to find a better supplier, figuring out how to market to a new customer base, or trying to streamline their innovation. Whatever the case, they're finding ways to find gaps and bridge them.

Problem-solving also comes in handy when you're trying to address risk, and there's a lot of risks involved in running a business. As human beings, we have developed a way of identifying trends and seeing cause-and-effect relationships in our environment. These skills enable us to anticipate where things may break in the future and deal with them before they plummet out of control. Problem-solving can be applied to such risks so that you take action today that influences the likelihood of things going wrong in the future.

You can also apply problem-solving skills to improve your performance and that of others. As entrepreneurs and businesses, we do not exist as islands. Our environments are complex and ever-changing, and so are the relationships that make them up. This means that the actions of one person will always affect someone else or will change an environment or its dynamics.

It's these interdependencies that allow us to work together to solve complex problems, but they also create a demand that everyone commits to continuous improvement, so they can adapt to the improvements others are making. Problem-solving helps us wrap our minds around those relationships and create the improvements and changes necessary to survive and compete in an ever-changing environment.

In cases when problem-solving is not about fixing what's broken or addressing risk, then it's about seizing an opportunity. It's about creating new innovations and changing the environment so that it becomes more desirable. It's problem-solving that allows us to identify and make use of the opportunities around us and exert a level of control over our future. Clearly, these skills are a critical part of daily life for everyone, but more so for business people. Defining and refining them can help you solve problems more effectively over time.

Solve a Puzzle, Solve a Problem

Puzzles are an excellent way to pass time with yourself. Whether that puzzle is a 3000-piece jigsaw, a Sunday crossword puzzle from the New York Times, or a 3D mechanical puzzle, it doesn't matter. All puzzles power your brain and help you develop your problem-solving skills.

Even though puzzles seem to have become more popular in recent days, they have a very long history. They existed in different forms even in the ancient world. People in Biblical times told riddles to each other. There are puzzle jugs that date back to 1700 BCE in Cyprus. China had magic squares in 700 BCE. People have always known how useful puzzles are in keeping the brain agile.

In our modern world, jigsaw puzzles are said to have been invented in 1767, crossword puzzles first featured in the newspapers in 1913, and the Rubik's cube was made in 1974. Whichever type, puzzles are incredibly beneficial. They exercise both sides of the brain.

Our brains have two hemispheres that control different functions. The left side deals with logical and analytical thinking, while the right side deals with creativity. As you work on puzzles, you engage both sides, giving the brain a proper mental workout.

Because of their nature, puzzles improve your memory. They reinforce different connections between our brain cells and allow the brain to form new ones, so that even our short-term memory becomes better. We use our memory when solving a Rubik's Cube or completing a jigsaw puzzle. We have to remember pieces, sizes, and shapes, and visualize the way everything fits together. Puzzles are an incredible way to improve our problem-solving skills for this same reason. You have to think critically in nearly every puzzle you solve, and that skill translates to real life.

Different puzzles require different approaches, and because of this, you have to do a lot of trial and error. You have to create theories and test them and then change tracks if things aren't working. It is as though you get to do everything you do when running a business, but this time in a controlled environment where the stakes are not as high.

What is more, solving puzzles will improve your attention to detail. As you're trying to solve the puzzle, you have to mind every detail. You have to train your eyes to see small differences in shape, color, and size so that you can bring everything together. This ability transfers to running a business where you need attention to detail to identify where exactly things are going wrong and work to make improvements.

It has also been said that puzzles improve your spatial and visual reasoning. As you solve a jigsaw puzzle, for example, you have to look at the individual parts of the puzzle or the spaces that are available in a crossword puzzle, and then figure out how to fit the pieces or words where they're supposed to be. If you solve a puzzle every day, for only 10 minutes, you will improve your spatial and visual reasoning skills which makes you better at daily tasks.

And you can do all this while improving your mood. As your brain puzzles over a riddle and solves it, dopamine is produced in the body, leaving you feeling amazing!

A Puzzle a Day Keeps Competitors at Bay

Set aside 10 minutes of your day to complete a puzzle of your choice. You can make this a period toward the end of your day to help you relax or in the middle of the day as you're trying to transition between business tasks. Simple puzzles like trivia, word and number searches, spot the differences, or sudoku will do the trick.

If you're feeling more adventurous, here are a few other types of puzzles that you can try out:

- Disassembly or assembly puzzles: Assembly puzzles asks you to put pieces together, while disassembly puzzle does the opposite. It asks you to take one thing and break it into different adequate pieces.

- Boggle solitaire: This is the solo version of a board game with the same name. You get letters in a grid, and you find as many words as you can.

- Brain teasers: This is a logic puzzle that doesn't necessarily need a pen and paper but exercises your brain anyway.

- Cryptograms: These are coded puzzles. You get a phrase, and each number is represented by a different number, symbol, or letter, and your job is to figure it out.

Other than these, there's a whole world of puzzles and games that can help you exercise your brain efficiently. Start with what excites you and resonates with you the most.

Chapter 13:

Plan Your Next Day to Stay Productive

As a business person, you need to understand and acknowledge the value of planning and preparation. A sports match with no game plan is just players fumbling on the field. A big event without the details fined out just results in chaos.

You probably have your long-term plans in place. You have a vision, and chances are you've taken the time to figure out the details. You probably can see in your mind what the next five years or 10 looks like for your business. Yet, the problem comes when you, like many of us, fail to prioritize the same kind of planning in your daily life.

You begin your morning without a clear plan, and you end up doing whatever things present themselves to you as urgent throughout the day. Unfortunately, that's not a good idea if you want to hit your big dreams. Starting your day without a plan sets you up for failure.

It's ridiculous that we set goals on the order of years and seasons, but it's the things that we do every day — our daily habits, the tasks we complete, and the things we give precedence to — that compound over time into failure or success. A couple of aimless days every month can cause you to lose progress toward important goals. Sure, one or two of those days are acceptable, but generally, when we have more days lived out unplanned than those lived with purpose, we're missing our goals. And it's only a matter of time before we ask where things went wrong with our goals, as they inevitably will.

The best defense against wasting time, against having busy and hectic and yet unproductive days, is to have a good offense.

That offense is a daily planning ritual. By setting aside only 10 minutes of your day to plan your next day, you make sure that you're always getting closer to your goals.

Make Planning a Habit

It has been argued that both motivation and inspiration are vital to running any business, but you can still be efficient without either of them. However, you can't be efficient without scheduling your habits. There's a degree of motivation that flows from action, so the things you choose to do every day can push you in the right direction with your ambitions. That's why it's so important to set aside those 10 minutes to plan your day.

There will be mornings when you wake up feeling motivated to seize your day, but there will also be days when you wouldn't feel like you're in the headspace to plan anything. In the latter kind of days, the plans that you've made in advance will carry you through. Create action plans that reflect your vision in advance, and your future self will thank you for it.

Making a planning ritual helps you get things done even when you're disengaged and tired. It helps you when you catch yourself longing for the end of the week rather than inhabiting the day. It returns you to your motivation. It guarantees that you approach every day with a plan. Set an alarm for your 10 minutes of planning at the same time every day. You can make this part of your daily shutdown ritual. To turn it into a habit conveniently, bundle it with an already existing habit, such as brushing your teeth before bed or listening to a podcast before lights out.

If you need to, rely on to-do list apps so you can create a recurring task for planning your next day. Alternatively, you can set it into an alarm on your phone. Habits come to us easier when we can see the results of our dedication immediately. Fortunately, planning your day is something that will pay off instantly. You'll notice that you feel more focused, organized, and motivated with a plan for how you'll spend the hours ahead.

With time, planning the day will become second nature to you. In the early days, if you catch yourself struggling to make it a habit, don't break the chain during the weekends. Rather than letting your weekends roll by, even if you're hoping for a laid-back day, plan it. Put your errands and dinner dates on your to-do list for Saturday and Sunday. Schedule your leisure, relaxation, and side projects.

For the best results, your to-do lists need to be built around your goals and ambitions. Make sure that each item in your daily plan is actually getting you closer to your bigger goals. Essentially, align your daily planning session and daily tasks with your objectives for the long term. To get started, break your big goals into smaller daily tasks. For example, if one of your long-term goals is to get in shape, as you're planning your day, you can schedule a 10-minute HIIT workout for yourself. Do this for both your professional and personal goals.

As a rule, if you catch yourself struggling to make your to-do list realistic, it could be a sign that you've lost sight of your goals, or that you have too many of them. Part of planning your day is to avoid overextending yourself or giving the bulk of your energies to things that don't count in the long run. On such days, you can begin your plan by doing an inventory of how you've been spending your time and what action you've been taking toward your goals.

Reconnect with your most important goals and make sure they're at the heart of your daily tasks.

As you plan your day, think of your week as a whole. You probably have many goals and different possible tasks that you could do to accomplish them. You also have limited time each day, and that's okay. There are goals that need daily action, and there are others that need to be worked on only twice a week, so you create enough momentum. Be sure you differentiate these.

That way, you don't get overwhelmed by everything you have to do. There are days you may want to do activities related to only one professional goal, and there may be others that you may work toward several goals. That's alright, as long as you're making progress in the right direction.

Always begin with the tasks that take you toward your goals and then add what you have to do at the end of your plan. Do not set your mandatory meetings and appointments first. Urgent deadlines, unless they were set by you and actually form part of your plan, do not go first. The plan is not to prioritize your life around other people's needs and demands on your time – it is to prioritize your days around your goals and then fit other people in. Putting your 'have-to-dos' last will help you arrange them around your goals instead of the other way around.

In an ideal world, we would only focus on the daily tasks that contribute toward our goals. The reality, though, does not permit that. We have obligations and commitments that need to be fulfilled, some of which don't really impact our business growth. Cull these obligations as much as you can; re-evaluate meetings that are recurring, delegate responsibilities that can be shouldered by others, and get comfortable telling people 'No.'

When you've done that, finish the 'have-to-dos' in your list with as much zest as you finish the other tasks.

Use a Productivity Method

A productivity method can help you structure your 10 minutes of planning. It can help you to keep your eyes on the important stuff, rather than getting caught up in the details. There are many popular productivity methods, but I'll share four of them that I've used intermittently. Experiment with them to find out the one that works best for you, even if that means adopting your own mix of them.

• Eat the frog

According to this method, you identify only one significant task for the day and then you deal with that one first. This method is a good option if you want to put your headlight to work early. Make sure that this task is something you would otherwise avoid.

Alternatively, you can make this task the one that feels way too big for you to deal with or the one you find uncomfortable. Go at it immediately before you give your brain a chance to postpone. As you plan your day, make sure you identify the 'frog' task so that it's at the top of your list of things to do.

• The Pomodoro technique

This technique is very good for you if you enjoy working in short sprints with breaks in between. It was developed in the 1980s by a struggling student who would set aside only 10 minutes to study with focused attention, using a Pomodoro shaped kitchen timer. To use this technique, have a timer. Set it for about 25 minutes or the span of time that works for you and give your whole attention to one task until the timer rings. When that session ends, record what you've finished and take a short break, about five minutes long. After three or four of these intervals, take a longer break.

To plan your day using this technique, estimate the number of work sessions you'll need, and account for the breaks. Assign a task for each session, and tick it off as you go about your day. This method will force you to think about the amount of time you give to each task and help you plan accordingly. You can opt to use it for your whole day or only for the most important tasks in your day.

• Time blocking

With this productivity method, you divide your day into different and clearly separate blocks of time. You could get as specific as stating 'between 9:30 am and 10:20 am' or simply saying 'morning', based on how long you estimate a task to take.

Then, you work without taking any breaks for the set time block until you complete the specific task or number of tasks.

Similar to the Pomodoro technique, you'll need to properly estimate how long you need to complete your tasks. Ensure that you set aside time blocks for things like breaks, commutes, and lunch. A lot of time, a task will take less time or more time than you expected. That's alright. Make modifications to your list quickly and continue through your day.

As time goes by, you'll get more proficient at estimating how long tasks take. In the meantime, double the time you imagine something will take and take it from there.

• The Eisenhower Matrix

This final productivity method throws a spanner in the works. It forces you to think about the importance and the urgency of your tasks rather than only tending to what feels the most urgent without asking whether it's crucial or not. It breaks down the tasks into four and prescribes a way to deal with each task based on where it falls. The tasks that you judge to be urgent and important have to be done immediately. The ones not important and not urgent should be added to your calendar. The urgent and unimportant tasks are to be taken off of your to-do list.

To begin planning your day using this method, list everything you hope to do in the day as you regularly would. Next, sort them into categories of *urgent and important, urgent and not important, not urgent and not important*, and *not urgent and important*. After your tasks fall into any one of these categories, you can go on and act on them as needed.

Delegate where necessary, take items off your list where you need to, schedule what you need to, and then begin your day with the most urgent and important tasks.

Stick to Your Daily Plan

Even with a very good plan and with the purest of intentions, there will be days when it's hard to finish everything on your to-do list in one day. Inevitably, we find that we've been drawn by distractions like online shopping and social media. Ad-hoc tasks delegated by other people can come up and interfere with our focus or force us to give our energies to things we had not planned.

Unfortunately, an interruption can snowball and make a series of unproductive days and aimless weeks.

Do not let it get to that. Commit to approaching each day with intention even when they don't always go exactly as planned. Even so, there are some things you can do to make sure that you stick to your daily plan, including the plan to plan your next day:

- ### Say no to distractions

Before you begin your day, commit to having zero distractions. If the bulk of your work is done on a computer or online, remove any desktop programs that you know will distract you. Switch off your phone if you need to. Turn down email notifications or set aside a part of your day for responding to emails, and stay off your email for the rest of the day.

- ### Keep track of your time

You track your budget so you're intentional with your spending, similarly, you should track your time to spend it most efficiently. Tracking your time can help you use it well. Use an automatic time-tracker app that gathers information about your usage of mobile devices and your desktop, sorting your time online into categories like 'neutral' and 'productive.'

- ### Regular check-in

You can apply mindfulness even to the way you spend your time. Regularly check in with yourself to see if you're going through your day according to your plan and with your focus being on the right things. One business coach suggests that you do these check-ins every hour and ask yourself whether you spent your last hour well. That way, you manage your time; it doesn't manage you.

- ### Adapt your plan

There are times when there will be unexpected tasks coming up throughout the day that you can't ignore. When that happens, flow with it. You'll only have a problem if you try to take on unplanned work without revising your earlier plans. The alternative is to make the unplanned work part of a new plan.

Take a moment when you realize that you have to go off-task to readjust your daily plan. Make sure you note the to-do items that you'll need to reschedule, so that you can do that when planning the next day, and then work with your new plan. You can always leave an extra hour from your daily plan to allow you to take on any unplanned tasks, or at the very least, to make corrections as you need to if the day doesn't play out as you hoped.

Once you've made planning your next day a habit, used a productivity method to make the plan, and made your long-term goals actionable in the short term, you can begin having productive days which add up to more meaningful weeks, months, and then years.

However, don't let this process become reflexive. Once in a while, take some time out to think about your approach to daily planning and whether it's helping you do more or if it has become redundant. You have a monthly review to consider whether your daily planning sessions are working or whether they need to be corrected or even overhauled for better techniques. Ask yourself questions like:

- How am I spending my days? Are they intentional and calm or haphazard and stressful?

- Do I feel like I've accomplished my goals at the end of most days?

- Do I complete the majority of my to-do lists or skip more?

- Am I still on track toward my goals?

By being honest about how your days are playing out, you can start fine-tuning your daily planning sessions so that they yield better results. You'll realize that hectic days mean that you prioritize better or find someone to delegate some tasks to. Missing planning sessions may mean that your productivity techniques, for example, are not working for you and that you need a better approach.

If you're not making progress toward your goals, it means that you're not planning enough intention or frequency for them in your days. Whatever the problem, work to resolve it by changing how you run your daily planning session.

It's not unheard of to need to experiment a lot and try a number of combinations and iterations for daily planning before you find a method that actually helps you do more. As you plan your day, don't aim for perfection. Instead, aim for progress. Aim for flexibility and consistency. While I have provided tactics and tips to help you make the planning effective, there's no one size that fits all. Rather, we feel better prepared to face our days when we are consistent.

You can simply show up today and trust that a series of productive days will create productive weeks. As you chip away at your to-dos with focus and intention every day, there's no limit to the things you can do.

Chapter 14:

Learn a New Skill to Stay Adaptable

What things do you need to learn to stay relevant as a business person?

This is a tricky question to answer because technologies are always changing. Businesses come and go, and even when they stay, they have to change their way of operating and their processes. Predictions turn out wrong.

Still, that's a question worth thinking about, both for the professional benefits of learning a new skill and the sheer joy of acquiring new information. Here I'll help you see what you stand to gain from setting aside only 10 minutes of your day to learn a new skill, beyond acquiring the skill itself. I'll also provide some suggestions for skills you can begin with. The options for the things you can learn are endless, and your capacity to learn is way more than you can imagine. All you need to do is stay consistent, and you'll see the results.

Some of the skills I've provided in my list of suggestions are more useful for some businesses than others, but all of them will be beneficial. Besides being work-related, they also help make your life better, regardless of what line of business you're in. Some of them will take a week with only 10 minutes of practice every day, while others will take a longer period to grasp.

Even so, learning a new skill is a good way to get out of feeling stuck when you get to such points in life. Learning a new skill gives you motivation. It can sometimes be the kick you need to begin your day energetically. When you're an expert at everything you do, daily tasks can start to feel lifeless. Learning a new skill reminds you that there's still a lot more that you could learn and become.

It can give you joy, energy, and a sense of purpose. It helps to beat the boredom of repetition. Repeating the same things every day can be draining, while trying a new thing that requires more effort than your habitual actions can be inspiring.

It helps you feel better about yourself when you're able to engage in a new skill and work your way until you master it. You gain courage and confidence, which you need to override anxiety and fear. You feel more empowered by the mere attempt to learn something new, which also keeps you healthy. We're all in a sense fighting against time. As you age, your brain gets older as well. Learning a new skill helps your mind reshape itself. It keeps the brain young even with the passage of time.

Most importantly, learning a new skill keeps you flexible. By making sure that you're continually a student and trying new things, you learn that you're capable of growth and change. This keeps you open to new opportunities in business and in life. Any business person who doesn't learn new skills is destined to wither mentally and physically. They're bound to fall victim to the same mindsets and habits that have held them back over and over again.

Make Your 10 Minutes Count

Set aside 10 minutes out of your day and commit that time to learning a new skill. Make sure that the skill you choose is something that is meaningful to you. More than learning styles, one thing that gets in the way of learning is attempting to learn things you don't care about. To do well as a student, you need to find meaning in your learning.

A study done in 2003 by Simon and Chase proves this point well. In the first part of the study, researchers showed expert and amateur chess players a chessboard arrangement from an ongoing game. They were each asked to remember the position of the different pieces.

The amateurs who were playing could hardly remember any of the positions of the pieces, but the experts were able to recall the majority of them. This is because experts are able to see the strategy, and they understand the meaning behind any one of the pieces being where it is. Then, researchers proceeded to the second part of the study during which they showed amateurs and experts boards with the chess pieces arranged randomly, and they asked each of them to recall the positions. Both groups performed the same. This time, because the experts couldn't find any real meaning or connection in the arrangement of the pieces, they couldn't remember their positions.

The case is the same for learning. When we were in school, we learned different figures and facts, but how many do we actually remember? The only information that you'll remember is information that is meaningful to you. It's the information that you can connect to your own experiences and to your life. As you're learning a new skill, if you try to simply memorize facts at random, chances are that you will forget them. It'll be like all those times in school you tried to memorize a formula without understanding why it matters.

So to make the skill stick that you pick up, make sure it's something you're truly interested in and something with real-life connections. You need the ability to see it fit in with a larger scheme of things. The next time you take a class in money management, rather than memorizing formulas, understand the relevance of each of them and see how it will benefit you. You'll see how much faster you grasp concepts.

In the same vein, make sure that you're learning by doing. As people, we learn best when we're able to do the tasks we're learning. Regardless of your IQ or how well you perform academically, most of your learning happens once you start applying the lessons you read about. If, for example, you're trying to understand SEO so that you can market your business better, rather than spending all your time learning the theory and the language, dive into practice as soon as you can and allow yourself to try and fail. Begin a blog and write some posts. Optimize them and find out first-hand what's working and what's not. As you practice, you learn more.

Throughout the learning process, maintain a sense of curiosity. Nothing is more capable of stimulating learning than curiosity. Ask questions. Allow yourself to make mistakes. Let things get messy if that's necessary. Rather than just relying on the textbook or the course curriculum that you're using to guide you, take the lead. Look for answers from many places. Don't just try to memorize techniques and theories – question each step to understand it.

Think about the reasons behind each step. Tinker with the knowledge and the tools you have available to you, and see how much you end up discovering. You may find that you even surpass your own expectations.

Skills to Get You Started

Here are some skills that you can begin developing. The idea is to take 10 minutes each day and keep up developing one skill until you master it well enough before moving on to the next one.

- **Basic writing skills**

Even if you're not a writer by profession, you still have to write – whether that's an email to your team, a proposal for a new project, or a request for funding. Even texting a friend counts as writing. You do well in learning how to communicate your ideas well when writing. It will make your life and work easier. You don't even have to get a degree in English. You can simply take a course in business communication.

- **Digital literacy**

If you ask many people what kinds of digital skills they would love to learn, chances are they'll say things like 'programming' or 'website development'. Those are great skills to learn, but they're not all you can learn when it comes to the digital world.

Everyone could definitely benefit from having a good enough degree of digital literacy. You need to be able to use your computer, for example, to its fullest skills. Some of the computer skills you can learn are: how to touch type, how to use software such as Slack, how to manage your email inbox, how to collaborate on projects through Microsoft 365 or Google Suite, how to use task management software, keyboard shortcuts that can save you time on routine tasks, and so forth.

If these skills sound elementary to you, that's a good thing. It means you're ahead of the curve, but you still have a lot more to learn. If you're not sure about some of them, you now know where to start. Basic digital literacy helps you run your business better. It frees up your time so you can focus on the more important work tasks.

• Reasoning and logic

Logical thinking is an extremely powerful tool for problem-solving and decision-making. However, many of us never imagine we need any training in this area. It's worth it to spend some of your time learning how to think logically and to understand the kind of cognitive biases you're prone to, and how to avoid them.

For clarity, I'm not recommending pure robot-like logic. That would only serve to alienate you from your friends and yourself. Still, you need logical thinking in your toolbox to run a business well.

• How to conduct job interviews

Job interviews are something we all have to do in different forms. If you run your own business, chances are you'll be the one interviewing someone. While that may not be the most fun activity, you can still make the interview process more positive and less stressful for the interviewee. You can take some time to learn the art of interviewing so you don't end up conducting the interview like an uncomfortable interrogation.

A good interviewer knows how to put the interviewee at ease. They know how to make the environment conducive for the kind of conversation that would help them determine whether someone is a good fit. Learn how to do interviews in person and over digital media, like on the phone.

- ## Taxes

Unless you were so lucky as to go to an incredibly practical school, it's probable that you didn't learn how to do your taxes. Yet, that's something we all have to do, so you'll do well to learn how they work, both on a personal and a corporate level. I'm not suggesting that you manually fill out and file all your forms, even though you can do that if you have the time. I'm simply saying that it's a good thing to understand what's happening in the background of the software you use for tax preparation.

That way, if you ever need to hire an accountant, as someone who knows how to do their taxes, you'll be able to choose someone who is competent. As it is, taxes are a bit complicated, especially if you own your business, but the basics are simple enough. Enroll in a course that will give you a general overview to start with.

Chapter 15:
Discipline is the Glue for Habits

The first American on Everest, Jim Whittaker, is credited with the saying, "You can never conquer a mountain. You can only conquer yourself." This saying is as much true for climbing mountains as it is for forming habits.

Imagine an HR manager in a company. Let's call her Marietta. Every morning, Marietta gets up before everyone else to exercise. Then she gets ready and shows up at the office, where she works efficiently, avoiding distractions and giving all her attention to high-value projects. At the end of the day, she attends an online class, and she'll be getting her Ph.D. in a few months.

Do you know someone like Marietta? How can people like her do so much, so consistently? And how can you achieve as much in your business and personal life as they do?

Part of the answer lies in self-discipline. It's the discipline that pushes us to keep working on our goals and aspirations, even when we're not feeling like it. Self-discipline allows us to put off immediate pleasure and comfort in the short term, as we pursue long-term gain. If you're capable of sacrificing temporary satisfaction and enduring hardships for the sake of your long-term goal, that counts as self-discipline. It requires you to step out of your comfort zone, because nothing and nobody ever grows in the comfort zone.

In 2009, the *European Journal of Social Psychology* found that it takes between 18 and 254 days to form a new habit. According to the study, it takes the average person 66 days to make a new behavior automatic. Ultimately, it depends on the kind of habit you're trying to form. The study listed a range of variables involved in habit formation that make the range so big. Some habits take longer to form. In the study, many participants found it easier to start habitually drinking a glass of water before breakfast than doing 50 sit-ups every morning.

There's a common myth that you only need 21 days to build a new habit. The idea can be traced back to the 1960s after Dr. Maxwell Matz published a book, where he referenced the number as a metric he used for himself and his patients. As the book became more popular, his observation was accepted by the general populace as fact. Even so, the 21 days fall within the range of 18 to 254 days, so it can be related to the findings earlier referenced in the chapter.

During this period of habit formation is when you most need self-discipline. This is the time when you need to keep showing up against all odds until your 10-minute action becomes automated.

There may not be a one-size-fits-all when it comes to the time frame for forming different habits, but if you keep showing up consistently, whatever action you're working on will inevitably become a habit. Discipline is both the fuel and the glue that makes habits stick. I like to think of discipline as training in the gym. Some people will not take up any weights because they're afraid or they doubt that they can lift a certain amount. Some people won't reach for the stars, while others will, so often that they overachieve due to their strong will. Which team do you want to belong to?

There will be an element of discipline needed at the beginning of each 10-minute action because essentially, what you do will be drawing a line in the sand as you try to kick out some old habits. Then, it'll take continuous discipline to keep performing the same execution every day after that.

Persist Till You Reach Your Goals

By definition, self-discipline is the ability to keep moving forward, staying motivated, and taking continuous action no matter how you feel emotionally or physically. You're being self-disciplined when you intentionally choose to keep going after something that makes you a better person, and you do it in spite of the unfavorable odds. It has to do with mastering the willpower to persist and follow through with your intentions.

It's the discipline that will push you to do that 10-minute HIIT session even when you don't feel like it. It gives you the strength to plan your next day so that you stay productive, even when you're ready to give up. It helps you stick with your journaling practice until you gain clarity. Self-discipline helps you move toward success despite what others would call insurmountable odds.

Admittedly, we're not born self-disciplined, but we can definitely cultivate discipline. You can embrace daily practice and repetition that will grow and improve your discipline. You can change how you think about your willpower. If you believe yourself to be limited in your willpower, you probably won't surpass that limit. If you believe that you cannot keep up your 10-minute actions, then your belief will become self-actualizing. You may as well not begin.

The first step to achieving everything you're hoping for is believing that you can. Embracing a mindset of unlimited willpower will keep you disciplined. It'll make sure that you continue growing and becoming more resilient. In short, your internal conceptions about your self-control and willpower will determine how disciplined you stay. If you can remove your internal obstacles and truly believe yourself to be capable, then you can achieve anything and everything.

Conclusion

One thing that's true of all successful people is that they have daily practices that are connected to mastering something that matters to them, and they perform these rituals each day with no exception. It's said of Jerry Seinfeld, the famous comedian, that he wrote one joke a day. He was so committed to this practice that it didn't matter to him whether it was a good joke or a bad one. The important thing was that he kept going. The habit of writing one new joke every day was non-negotiable to him.

As powerful as the daily rituals can be, the mistake most people make is that they don't have them. Whenever I address large groups of people, I find that only a maximum of 3% keep a consistent daily habit that actually adds to their long-term progress. When probed further, many people will say that they don't have enough time, and that's almost understandable. We're busier today than we've ever been, with our work, social, family, and private lives. The idea of adding yet another task to an already full schedule sounds unthinkable.

In this book, I've shared a different way of thinking – an approach that requires you to set aside only 10 minutes of your time per day on a habit you want to cultivate. With that approach, you can join the ranks of the small percentage of people who truly know the value of daily practice. If you choose to put this approach into practice, it can change your life for the best. With each one of the 13 habits I've discussed in this book, the point is not to do a lot, but to do a little each day, consistently. Discipline is the key.

You have to do something every day without exception. This alone will start creating a sense of congruence between how you behave and your identity. In other words, as soon as you start putting this principle to the test, you'll gain the certainty that you're the kind of person who's capable of being extraordinary. You'll start to get past the lie that excellence is something you're born with, and it will dawn upon you that excellence comes from hard work, discipline, and practice, and anyone can achieve it.

You just have to give up the convenient excuse of not having enough time, and you have to step out of your comfort zone.

Developing the habits from this book won't take you more than 10 minutes. You only need to slot in these 10 minutes to your schedule, and stick to it. It's as simple as that.

While doing the activity, whether that's HIIT, taking a walk in nature, yoga, meditation, reading, decluttering, solving a puzzle, or learning a new skill, figure out a way to maximize that time.

In the different chapters of this book, you have the tips and methods that will help you get started with this approach, and will keep you going on your journey, but only if you stay determined and dedicated. Use these methods well to make sure that your 10 minutes matter in the long haul.

I believe that this practice of incorporating only a few activities for 10 minutes into your daily life has incredible power to turn your dreams and goals into reality. All you have to do is be persistent and consistent. You'll see that these small steps toward healthy habits are the best investments you could make for your future success. They've worked for me, Lydia, and many more of my friends. And I know they'll work for you too!

THE END

Body & Mind Self-care Exercise

You can start from small goals to reach bigger ones, just a simple 10-minute walk a day can lead to reaching any health goals you have set for yourself!

Reminder

It can be a long journey, but in the end it will always be worth it and will train you to get used to a new routine

Meditate

Tidy up your space

Keep & write a gratitude jar

Start to set boundaries

Make a daily routine

djpinkney.com

HOW TO DEVELOP HABITS AND SHAPE YOUR LIFE WITH 10 MINUTE ACTIONS

About The Author

David is a passionate entrepreneur who is successfully building a Kindle Direct Publishing business.

He is excited to share his journey with other aspiring entrepreneurs looking to follow in his footsteps. Through hard work, determination, and a commitment to his craft, David has built a thriving business that he is proud of.

He hopes that by sharing his experience, he can inspire others to pursue their own entrepreneurial dreams and achieve success.

Little Steps to Big Achievement

Author Notes

I am a person that used to jump from one thing to the next, I would always start something and most likely never finish it! This includes everyday things, like going to the gym, reading a book, learning a new skill, and so on!

Until I found out that doing the very same things each day for only 10 minutes could have a big impact on my life and help me to reach my goals. Instead of trying to go to the gym for an hour a day, I instead did a 10-minute HIIT workout, went on 10-minute walks, set a time limit to read for only 10 minutes a day

Little Steps to Big Achievement

Author Notes

By setting a time limit of 10 minutes, I was able to stick to each task and it didn't feel like a chore! Not only was I able to stick to each task and continue to do them daily, but I was also able to complete goals that I wouldn't have done in the past - even small things, like finishing a book.

I am now building an online informational and publishing business because I have learned that developing habits and shaping your life, actually starts by taking small steps first and by starting with 10-minute daily tasks, I can finally reach the goals I set for myself.

THANK YOU

LITTLE STEPS TO BIG ACHIEVEMENT

I just want to say a massive thank you
for reading my first book 'little steps
to big achievement' - I do really hope
that you found some useful
information within this book and in
some way it will help you to reach
any goals you have set for yourself.

D J Pinkney

djpinkney.com

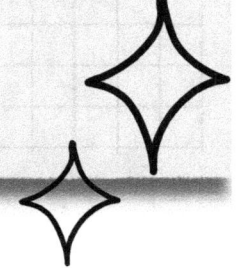

NEWSLETTER

Join my newsletter to stay up-to-date with my latest book releases, updates, messages, and so much more! Simply provide me with your email address and I'll make sure you never miss a beat. Sign up today and be the first to know about all my exciting new books, news, and offers.

Scan Here

Feedback

If you could spare a few minutes to leave
an honest review on Amazon, it will help
us to improve our books and service.
Thank You

Tell Us About Your Experience

Please let us know how you feel about this book, your feedback will help me to provide better books in the future.

How do you feel about this book?
Please rate this book on a scale of 1 to 5 stars and then share this rating on social media by taking a picture of this page & use the hashtag
#LittleStepsToBigAchievement

D J Pinkney

Little Steps to Big Achievement

VWG BOOKS
Independent Publisher

D J Pinkney

Little Steps to Big Achievement

VWGBooks is supported by you the customer, without you, we wouldn't be here, so on behalf of VWGBooks, I would just like to say a big THANK YOU for buying this book, we really hope you enjoy it.

We highly appreciate your feedback, which is always important to us.

If you could spare a few minutes to leave an honest review on Amazon, it will help us to improve our books and service.

VWG BOOKS
Independent Publisher